LITTLE SINS, BIG PROBLEMS

SARAH ONDERDONK

LITTLE SINS, BIG PROBLEMS

published by
✤ AMG *Publishers*

ISBN 0-89957-140-9

First printing—January 2003

Cover designed by ImageWright, Inc., Chattanooga, Tennessee
Interior design and typesetting by Reider Publishing Services,
    West Hollywood, California
Edited and Proofread by Judy Bodmer, Tricia Toney, Dan Penwell,
    and Sharon Neal

Printed in Canada
08 07 06 05 04 03 –T– 8 7 6 5 4 3 2 1

Thankfulness and Dedication

I thank the Lord for the special blessing of Todd . . . my best friend in Christ and the love of my life now and for eternity.

I am so thankful for my boys—John, Colin, and Daniel—you have given me joyful purpose and fast-tracked my quest to know God. How dearly I love and cherish you three.

I have been blessed by the love, creativity, and dedication of my original family: Mom and Dad, Tom and John, the late Katherine Kennedy, and Aunt Helen.

I am eternally grateful for the blessed empowerment of the Holy Spirit and the everlasting gift of God's written Word.

This book is dedicated to Jesus Christ
Who has been there for me in darkness and light.

Contents

Acknowledgments

Praise and deep gratitude to the following people for their inspiration and support: Warren Baker, Susan Berry, Stephen Board (*Writer's Edge Service*), Judy Bodmer, Nancy Carlson, Linda and Don Campanella, Nancy Edwards, Tonee and Jerry Edwards, Pastor Doug Freeman, Melinda and Don Groenemann, Ann Hardy, Denise Harris, Joy Jones Keys, Pastor Kevin and Marcy Lykins, Nancy Moore, Sharon Neal, Mendy Noble, Trevor Overcash, William Petty, Lori and David Pickle, Helen Pitts, Phillip Rodgers, Daryl Phillips, Tricia Toney, Dea Ward, Tim Way, Craig and Karen Whiting, friends at FCS, CHCS, CSA, and FC, and finally, my editor—Dan Penwell.

In memory of Professor James Carty, and my dear friend and mentor, Michael O'Malley.

Preface

I HAD JUST crossed the last "t" on a final draft of this book when the events of September 11 cast a dark and frightening shadow over our lives. The loss of that day shook me to the core and the world was instantly and irrevocably a very different place. In the immediate aftermath of terror, I put my book about sin to the side as I, like so many people I know, took a sobering look at what really matters. For a time, I had the feeling that the words and concepts wrapped around the subject of *little sin* had distant relevance to a world burnished with evil.

I would soon return to the premise of this book with even greater conviction because I realized that sin has roots and that its run of devastation takes a cumulative toll. Just as small droplets of rain over time can erode strong banks of land, everyday sins serve to corrode and deteriorate our relationship with God. Over a lifetime, the rain of sin, no matter how small it may seem, becomes a fount of poison to our soul.

I've heard more than one theologian suggest that perhaps God has removed His protective hand from our nation because we have turned from Him and, as a society, have become immersed deep in sin. I don't know if this is true, but I do believe that we, as a Christian people, must stand and fight for our very survival in these dangerous, uncertain times. We need the spirit of God and the force of goodness at the center of our collective heart. Recognizing sin in our midst is an important step toward ensuring that goodness prevails.

So it is with immense hope and praise to the Lord, through Whom all things are possible, that I offer you . . . *Little Sins, Big Problems*. I pray that it might open your eyes, touch your heart, and bless your life.

Author's note: Some personal names used in the book have been changed to respect the privacy of certain individuals.

Introduction

THERE WAS a "break-through-the-clouds" moment in my Christian walk that occurred at a local grocery store near a bin of green peppers. Strange, but true.

I'd carefully strapped my three boys, ages four, two, and one, into a toddler cart, and we were slowly cruising the produce aisle. It was spaghetti night, so I began sifting through a bin of green peppers in search of the firmest, freshest specimen. The vegetables were all freshly sprayed and dewy. I spied what I thought was the prize pepper and reached deep into the bin to retrieve it. Suddenly, it slipped out of my hand and landed on top of my shoe. In an act that defied natural physics, the pepper then projected off my foot and rolled violently across the freshly waxed supermarket floor. I watched with astonishment as the thing picked up speed. It was as if Pele in his prime had just booted it. The pepper continued to scoot along the floor until it lodged under a refrigerated unit of misty lettuce heads. I glanced around to see if anyone had noticed my carelessness. Fortunately, it was early in the morning and it was just the boys and me.

"Hang on," I said to my cart mates. "I'm gonna go get it."

The boys watched me sprint off in the direction of the hostage pepper. I knelt down to pick it up and, somehow, my spatially challenged mind did not account for a particular angle at which it needed to be yanked in order to extricate it. I gave it a bit of a tug upward and inadvertently smashed the thing. Now I was dealing not with a vegetable but pond scum.

"Oh, gross!" cried my oldest son, John, who had a clear shot of the pureed pepper and my swamp-thing hand.

"It'll be okay," I reported.

I looked down at the pepper, examined it a bit, and analyzed my options. Though I was cupping a bit of verdant sludge, the side that didn't get smashed appeared quite normal. It looked green and crisp. There wasn't a soul in sight. I could easily flip that slimy baby over, pop it back in the bin, clean myself up a bit, and move on to the onion bucket.

I stood there for a minute transfixed on that pepper.

"Mommy, what are you looking at?" John asked.

"The pepper," I replied.

"How come?" he asked.

"Because we're about ready to buy it," I said.

"But it's yucky!" he cried.

"Yes it is," I said, "but who else would want it?"

John thought for a moment. "No one," he said.

"That's right," I answered. "I dropped it. So I'm going to buy it."

So I bagged my mortally wounded vegetable, swept most of the green scum off my fingertips onto a tissue, and continued shopping. When it was time to check out, I had a déjà vu encounter with the checkout lady.

My cartons of milk, diapers, and egg noodles took an orderly procession down the conveyer belt. But when the cashier got to my pepper, she twisted up her face like a raisin and cried, "Gads! What happened to that pepper?"

"Hey Joe!" she called to the bag guy. "Get this lady another pepper, would ya? Gads!"

"No, no. That's alright," I said. "You see, I did that to it. I dropped it."

"Oh! Don't worry about it! We're gonna getcha another pepper," she insisted.

"But who's going to buy that one?" I asked her.

"No one!" she assured me.

"So I'll take it," I concluded.

We locked eyes for a moment and she looked at me the way a scientist examines a never-before-seen microbe. I felt quite sure this had never happened before on her shift.

I was also quite sure that there was more to this pepper incident than how to Cuisinart a vegetable without using a machine. I felt myself on the cusp of committing a "little sin." A seemingly harmless, benign act of "getting what the customer deserves!" In my thirty-nine years on the planet and untold grocery store visits, I'd seen dozens of people fold, spindle, and mutilate things in supermarkets. Invariably, I watched as those things went right back on the shelf. I'd even dropped a banana or two in my day and shoved them right back on the heap before moseying on to frozen foods. Meanwhile, some little old lady with cataracts could look forward to brown mushy stuff on top of her All-Bran the next day. Of course, I didn't get to the potential consequences in my mind at the time! But that day my eyes were opened wide to a world of "little sins" in my midst. And, all of a sudden, the little slips and skids around my day-to-day life were beginning to have a sharper feel to them. And they were becoming a lot less easy to just dust away as small and insignificant.

From Darkness to Light

1

FOR MOST OF my life, I've been kind of a "dietetic-cookie" Christian. My parents encouraged me to live a good, moral life. I could talk a bit about my faith, but underneath the crust, there wasn't much flavor or substance. Before God opened my eyes to the faceted prism of sin in my life, my thoughts and concerns rarely extended more than a few feet beyond where I happened to be standing at the time. I committed my life to Christ as a teenager. I believed in heavenly realms beyond what we know and see, but the spiritual me was consistently taking a back seat to the earthly me. As a young adult, I was obsessed with achievement. When I wasn't toiling at perfection, I was restless and bulleted with discontent. This

1

inward focus relegated the Lord to a place that was very distant from my daily life.

As a young single woman, I made fast strides up the communications ladder of a large corporation. In the late 1980s, after languishing for several years in a series of editorial, sweatshop jobs, I found work as a speechwriter for a large oil company. Working for a big business, I found there were plenty of opportunities to grow. The skills I acquired in "small pond" days had a direct and profitable application in my dealings with "bigger fish." In the corporate world, I quickly found my niche turning acronym-laden "company speak" into plain English. Mid-level managers liked the way I could write a simple, easy-to-deliver speech. I would use this skill to tunnel my way into increasingly higher paying and higher exposure positions. Over time, I was given opportunities to step beyond the realm of speech writing into deeper strategy areas. I began working with senior executives to develop organization-wide programs and was often consulted on broad communication issues. I traveled to lots of exciting places and met some interesting sports figures in professional auto racing, baseball, and football—headliners for promotions and sponsorships.

It was an exciting life . . . or so it might have appeared. But when the workday was done, I was inevitably holed up alone in a small townhouse feeling a bit like a castaway raft, alternately floating or sinking and all but consumed by the unpredictable seas of my life. I knew there was more to living than work. I just didn't know where or even what it was. I sought to fill that void with earthly panaceas like food.

My eating problems began in college. I was just out of the nest at seventeen, and thrust into the spin cycle of life away from protective parents and friends. It was then that I first turned to food to satiate something other than hunger. I used to take the money that my parents sent for "fun" and stock up on junk foods at the local grocery store. While my roommate and friends painted the town, I would often sit alone in my dorm room and gorge myself on snack foods. It didn't take long for my avarice to start showing up on my hips and face. And, in the absence of a solid and committed Christian core, I began to equate the loss of my looks with the dwindling sum of my entire worth. No amount of humor, intelligence, character, or anything *inside* could compensate for what was happening on the *outside*. When the mirror began telegraphing images of soft round cheeks and a padded jaw, I became unworthy inside and out. My soul had muted the volume on God, and there was little depth to me beneath what could be seen. I was all about surface. And that part of me was coming undone and pulling at the threads on the inside.

Others reinforced this negative, worldly view. When my college boyfriend, a handsome foreign exchange student, pinched me on the cheek one day and called me *gordita*, I didn't need a translator to tell me what he meant. I first met Edward as I was starting my college career. I was then a size six. Seven months later I was busting the seams of size-fourteen jeans. My sense of self-worth had begun a downward float like confetti in the air.

I completed my freshman year of college and was too discouraged to return in the fall. So I was back up the tree in the nest, commuting to a hometown university from my parents' house. While my first brush with the realities of living away from protective parents was harsh, the new reality of a return to parental boundaries and rules was worse. The college experience had whetted my appetite for parties that boiled over into wee hours. I was now subject to curfews and incendiary encounters with my mother in moonlit doorways at two o'clock in the morning. Home had become a battle zone. Worse still, I was miserable in my own skin. The mirror was showing me things I didn't like, and it was painfully apparent to me that heads no longer tilted my way. The irony was that I had become both large and small.

If I could only be attractive again, I thought, the hole in my soul could be patched and my life would be perfect. I'd get a boyfriend. We'd go to clubs and dance. On Sundays, we'd fill up on champagne at brunch. I'd get a job as a receptionist somewhere and make enough money to rent an apartment. Life would be full of fun. But it all came down to this . . . I had to be *thin*.

One day I overheard two family members talking about a young woman who was throwing up food in the toilet to lose weight. My relatives were revolted, of course, but I would have come close to selling my soul to get back into a skinny pair of jeans. While the thought of voluntarily throwing up food struck me as a crackbrain idea and extreme, I was open to its potential as a solution for me. That night, I stuck my finger down my throat and flushed about two thousand calories down the toilet. I would repeat this act almost nightly for the next several weeks. And, to my amazement, my body began to shrink. It was magic!

At the outset of my eating disorder, there were few outward manifestations of the disease. Apart from the fact that I was losing weight, I looked healthy and vibrant. But as I continued down this dangerous path, my body began to fight what I was doing to it. Though my figure was slimming, my face began to bloat. Most mornings, I would emerge from bed with moon slivers for eyes, and pillows of soft skin hiding my jaw. This was my body's way of trying to hold onto the fluids and nutrients I was flushing down the toilet each night. There were days no amounts of matte make-up or under-eye concealer could cover me up. The mirror was once again the enemy.

There was an infinitely larger problem beyond the reflection in the glass. I now had a condition—I was bulimic. This disease had me hooked. Like an alcoholic needing a bottle or a heroin addict craving a needle, I needed to fill my stomach with food . . . and I needed to get rid of it. I had crossed the threshold from simple experimentation with a strange, new weight-loss technique and had fallen into the dark, binding realm of addiction.

A year later, I left home again to return to the college I had attended as a freshman. My friends marveled at the "new me" and the boys began to take a second look. In a year's time, I had essentially shrunk. When asked to explain the big change, I shrugged it off as a change in diet and an inexplicable turbo-charge to my metabolism. The truth was, I was living a dark and potentially deadly secret life.

The madness would go on unabated for thirteen years. Though I lived this nightmare, the duration and depth of my sickness still remains staggeringly hard for me to believe years later. Truly, I am blessed to be alive.

An ironic and frightening aspect of this illness was the way in which it never once blocked or delayed life's achievements. I graduated from college and went on to excel in every job I ever had. My outwardly positive nature masked a rather sizable underlying crack in my self-esteem. My friends called me "Miss Congeniality." This is one of the cruel and deceptive aspects of bulimia. A person can be fundamentally ill and continue to shine in other areas, effectively throwing off track anyone trying to tune into the problem and help.

It's fair to say I was spiritually adrift during all of the years of my illness. My obsession with work and the secret sickness that gripped me left little time for bonding with God. I did pray from time to time. I remember many pitiful and desperate "why me?" petitions to God. There were nights when tears fell down my face in torrents. I also remember angrily throwing myself to the floor a few times, kicking, screaming, and just begging God to deliver me from my sickness. My heart was filled with bitterness and a sense of stolen entitlement. I blamed God for allowing the bulimia to go on. My prayers continued unanswered. The grip of madness was all over me, something I can only imagine is on par with being possessed. I hated and feared food, but it was something I simply couldn't avoid. If I wanted to live, I had to eat. All day long, there were periods when everything stops for food—breakfast, lunch, and dinner. There were office birthday parties, holiday gatherings, dinners out with friends, and Sunday supper with my parents. Every encounter with a meal brought me face-to-face with the disease.

I had tried many times over the years to break the cruel cycle of bingeing and purging. I would go for a few days and succeed at keeping the food down. I remember the "healthy" days as time spent fixating on the next meal. Every bite of food would threaten to trigger a purge. I knew at the outset of these purge-free periods that I would ultimately fail. Indeed, I always did.

During this long period of sickness, I had few close friends and a couple of failed relationships. My disorder forced me into exile; I didn't want anyone to get too close. Only one friend, Alan, knew what I was doing to myself. At one point I was engaged to him. He had been a very dear childhood friend. When we grew up, we thought our fondness for one another would make for a lasting happy-ever-after. It turned out we were wrong about that, but his friendship remained like a rock to me through the worst of my darkest days. He was the only one I trusted enough to confide in. I knew he would keep my secret; I knew I could count on him to be there for me.

Alan took me to support groups. He coached me on nutrition and exercise. He worked with my parents to plug me into a psychiatrist. The doctor was a gentle, grandfatherly man who helped me feel free to talk about my problem without fear of judgment, but he didn't give me an easy way out. I never went back. I chose, unwisely, to live with my illness. It was a foolish and reckless decision that undoubtedly cost me many years of good health and should have, by all earthly accounts, ended tragically. Had I sought the help of Christian counseling in the beginning, I have every reason to believe my stay in hell could have been commuted much earlier. But this was not the way it would play out for me. My days of darkness would number nearly five thousand.

I began most days with a throbbing headache and a weakness that made it literally hard to get out of bed. Yet, I managed to function well in the workaday world and keep my secret closely guarded. I became very learned about my disease. I turned to kitchen alchemy, first thing each morning, trying to undo what I had done the night before. I mixed vitamins and juices into exotic brews to replenish my body with the minerals and nutrition that I was flushing down the toilet every night. I took up a vigorous exercise program to sweat out the fluid that my body was desperately trying to hold in balance. Between the vitamins, the exercise, and a good swipe of makeup, I was able to hide the outward, physical manifestations of my disease. Despite what was going on inside my body, I looked healthy. However, I was playing a deadly game of roulette on a self-designed antidote path that was anything but sound or scientific.

I remember the time I plied myself with too many iron tablets. I lost feeling in my hands and feet while my hair started falling out in long brown strands. Other unpleasant side effects included muscle weakness, cramping from potassium deficiency, and near-constant dehydration. The wrong vitamins combined with strenuous aerobics could have stopped my heart cold. But God had a different plan.

Something of a truly supernatural nature happened to me in 1994 on a sweltering August afternoon in my suburban Virginia townhouse. It was an event that would forever sear in my heart and mind the living, palpable nature of a personal God.

Some months before, I had met the man who would become my husband. I knew right away that he was the one. He was the smartest person I'd ever met. He was strong, very attractive, a wonderful listener, and he could make me laugh. For a few weeks after we first met, my bulimia went into a short remission. But after a couple of months, I was back at it. We became engaged, but the excitement and stress propelled me into an accelerated phase of bingeing and purging.

A few months before my October wedding, I went to the Lord in prayer. I acknowledged the mess I'd made of my life and prayed for forgiveness for the sin of my slow-drip suicide through food. I thanked God for bringing me a stable, true love. I prayed to Him to give me a higher purpose in life that would pull me out of my earthly pit. I could no longer point my finger sideways or behind me or up to God in search of someone else to blame. I had a responsibility and accountability for myself and, this time, I was committed to changing my ways.

I felt a connection to God this time. My eyes were squinted tightly and my hands were clasped in prayer. Suddenly, I felt a tingling sensation; a kind of heaviness enveloped my right hand. It was as if my left hand was forcefully and uncontrollably squeezing my right hand. The sensation was both internal and external to me. To this day, I believe it was the Holy Spirit assuring me that the Lord was there and I was about to be free.

There was a powerful assuredness that took hold at that moment. I'd tried so many times before to break the chokehold of my disease. But it was always with a bodement of failure for I would stop the cycle only to purge again and again. This time it was simply different. I knew beyond a doubt that I would never again throw up food at will. Dirty water and tears would never again rain down my face. I was suddenly and miraculously strong.

It was over.

For the first time in nearly thirteen years, I was now able to resist and overcome these dark, uncontrollable temptations. I was no longer cowering in the shadows of a force that was compelling me to self-destruct. It was as if God turned on the light and the shadows simply went away.

People have asked me to speculate why I think God finally redeemed me after so many years of prayer and petition that seemed to go unanswered. What was the breakthrough? I have asked myself this question many times. While I can't say for certain, I do believe that God has a plan for our lives and a timetable for milestones along the way. Perhaps I was simply at a place where God knew that I had learned something valuable from hard, painful lessons in life. I was now ready to mature spiritually on His terms.

I heard a once-popular actress describe her own battle with bulimia as never really being finished. She described it as something that would always be a part of her life. I have heard others say much the same thing. From my own perspective, this is only partially true. While my history is part of the fabric of who I am, and it has greatly shaped my perspectives, my life as a bulimic is truly light-years behind me. When I think about those dark and hopeless days, it's almost as if I am recounting the story of someone else's life. My life today is full of joy and hope, because I have been restored, redeemed, and know firsthand that all things are truly possible with God.

If I had one thing to say to others who suffer from anorexia or bulimia, it's that God can heal you . . . completely. He will work through people in your life to make this happen—Christian counselors, pastors, parents, teachers, support groups, and friends. My own big mistake was failing to embrace the people God had strategically placed in my path much earlier, namely the mental health professionals I avoided. Still I would say with rock-solid conviction (my life as testimony), that there is hope for peace, health, and happiness if this disease is surrendered to God. Trust Him to ultimately carry you. I would also urge you to reach out and grab opportunities to lean on others as you fight to regain control of your body and soul.

Where am I today in my relationship with food? I try to eat a good, balanced, low-fat diet for health's sake. I'm also comfortable indulging in some of the "junk" foods once or twice a week with my husband. These occasions are a source of enjoyment and fun for me because I no longer fear food or worry about its ability to enslave me.

I am occasionally reminded of earlier days. Usually the reminders come when foods that were once "forbidden" are offered at unconventional times, such as the birthday cake that comes my way at a preschool party at nine o'clock in the morning. When I was a bulimic, a piece of cake passing by would literally make me sweat. Today, I am reminded of the anxiety of those moments and how a single piece of cake could trigger an internal tidal wave of torment. Praise God, a piece of cake at nine o'clock in the morning today is just a piece of cake. The memory remains, but the pain and destructive impulses are gone.

I've wondered over the years why God saw fit to save me at all. I certainly hadn't done much with my life up to the point when He miraculously intervened to bring healing. How would I use this gracious gift from God? As the door slammed shut on a painful passage in my life, God seemed to have something different in sight for me.

The Seeds of
Enlightenment

2

THERE'S A small creek at the base of the Blue Ridge
Mountains in Virginia where crystal water bubbles up
and flows through an obstacle course of rock and
stones. I don't know where this body of water begins or where
it ends. But there's a point where these stones, which have piled
up and shifted over hundreds and maybe thousands of years,
have erected a barricade that makes the water's passage suddenly very difficult. When the water hits this barricade, it stops
briefly. Then the water curls to the left and gushes white foam
out of a small, narrow passageway. The force of this liberated
rushing water appears far greater than the force exhibited

before it hit the rocks. Somehow the stones that held it back inevitably and powerfully also pushed it forward.

I think of this creek as a metaphor for the trials that slow us down and hold us back in life; and how God will maneuver us around these roadblocks and set us on a course that is infinitely more powerful and sure. When the Lord liberated me from the bonds of bulimia, He not only set me on a new course, but He also began working in my life to turn my past sufferings into strengths.

Still it took me awhile to get on God's track. With my eating disorder behind me and the wedding bells about to ring, I felt a bit like someone emerging from a deep freeze. The world looked different. Everything was better, brighter, and blooming with possibility. I wanted to see and feel and soak in the rays of goodness I'd never fully experienced as an adult. Though I harbored a soul-deep gratitude to God for what He had done for me, I didn't immediately change the fundamentals of my life. I didn't have some great reawakening experience and plunge 20,000 leagues deep into the holy waters of the Christian faith. I knew the Holy Spirit was working inside of me; I felt the presence of the Lord. I sensed that there was something undone and required of me, but the bright light of my new life blinded me. Once again, God took a backseat to earthly living. My focus and my interests were someplace else.

I met my future husband, Todd, at work. We bumped into each other in the hall on occasion. When he finally asked me out, I said "yes." At some point he kissed me. And that was it. It was like someone sprinkled fairy dust all over my head. Right away I knew that Todd was the man, and that God's hand was all over this relationship. We were married in 1994, nine months after our first date. I was thirty-three years old; Todd was forty. I was four months liberated from a crippling addiction . . . and my spirit was about to take flight.

After we were married, Todd moved into my suburban Washington townhouse. He sold his house in a neighboring city and we set about building our nest. After about twenty car trips back and forth, the merger of two households was complete. As we unpacked his things, I remember thinking that Todd came into the union with a lot of books—a lot of books about Christianity. We'd dated for nine months and, of course, I knew he was a follower of Christ and that he took his beliefs seriously. But I didn't have any appreciation for the depth of his faith until I began shoving aside cookbooks and celebrity biographies to accommodate his religious titles.

Leafing through some of Todd's books one day, I realized that God had given me a great and lifesaving gift. It was with a sense of shame that I began to understand that I hardly knew the Lord. I had become a believer as a teenager. I knew that Christ was both out there somewhere and at the same time inside of me. He had worked a miracle in my life. Yet, my knowledge of the Lord and my understanding of the Bible were shamefully poor. When I saw Todd's library of books about God, I realized that I had been a lazy student. This bothered me.

It wasn't until after the birth of our first son that I began to search aggressively for a stronger understanding of the Lord and His will for my life. I had appealed to Him before and He had answered my prayers. Now with a baby in my arms—a new soul to help grow and nurture—I had a growling hunger to know what it was I believed and why.

There's something about motherhood that stripped away the layers of "me" and made me realize that I'm responsible and accountable for raising up another human being to . . . gasp! . . . adulthood. A human being that I loved with a depth and passion that I never knew existed. I know that many a mother begins an extended, painful process of bargaining with God to live long enough to get Junior through college. It goes something like this:

> Dear God, I know I've been really rotten to scads of people in my life. I've been selfish and vain. I've been utterly and disgustingly appalling. But, dear God, I'll change my ways. I'll mend those fences. I'll walk the straight and narrow. Just, *please, please, please* . . . let me

be there to raise my kids. I don't want to get cancer. I don't want to get hit by a municipal bus. I need to live. God, let me live.

I had a lot of conversations like that with God when I was a new mother, but at some point I went beyond the one-dimensional petitions to embrace the broader scope of what it means to truly walk with God. At some point, I crossed over from being a bystander to being a participant in the search to learn more about my faith. I needed biblical and spiritual knowledge beyond the weekly church experiences.

I began making passionate petitions to God and searched earnestly in the Word for life's true purpose to be revealed. What I came up with in a matter of days . . . not months, not years, but days . . . was some life-changing insight into where I was *messing up!* I discovered there was room for major improvement. Though I had come out of a thirteen-year battle with bulimia and made sweeping changes in my life, I was still in the grip of something that threatened to logjam my spiritual walk.

Through the Word and the Holy Spirit's unmistakable tug at the heart, God revealed to me my "little sins." The quiet, insidious moral traps that were keeping me two steps behind an intimate walk with God. As I came face-to-face with my own daily shortcomings, I became aware of the "little sins" of others. There was suddenly a new awareness and sensitization that took hold of me that had never before been a part of my life. I could see with crystal clarity that sin is everywhere and it's often silent and veiled. It may be nothing more than an off-hand comment or a blind eye to a harmful deed. The traps are right in front of us and we don't see them. We plow right into them every day, and oftentimes, we don't even know we've been snagged. And yet we have sinned!

Then God went a step further in his dealing with me. He showed me that there's no such thing as a "little sin." This revelation rocked my world.

A Great Awakening

3

GOD HAD SEEN fit to deliver me from a life-threatening illness. I was now married to a man who would challenge me to further my connection with God. I had become a mother whose hands were vested with the awe-inspiring privilege and challenge of leading little ones to a life of joyful fulfillment in the Lord. Suddenly I was hungering for Biblical wisdom. I pushed my *People* magazines aside and began picking up the Bible every night, which is not something that happened too often before. Growing up in a Christian home, I could find my way around the books of the Bible, but that was about it. I'd read portions of the New Testament. I knew that John followed Luke and that Mark followed Matthew.

But, beyond the navigational logistics and what I could remember about classic Bible stories from childhood—Noah and the Ark, the life of Moses, and the stories of Jesus—I was pretty much biblically illiterate. So I prayed passionately to God for some guidance. One night, I came upon a verse in Proverbs that practically blew me across the room.

Bedtime was approaching. I was rocking quietly in my nursing chair. The boys were fast asleep. I began leafing through the Scriptures. Somehow I landed in Proverbs where I came across a thought-provoking verse that used the word *hate* to describe seven things that God abhors. I quit rocking and sat up a little straighter in my chair as I scrolled down this list very carefully. Anything that God hates is not something I wanted to see in myself. As one might guess, the things that God hates are the egregious acts like murder and base wickedness. What stunned me were the things mentioned right up front. Top billing on a list of things that God finds most detestable is . . . are you ready for this? . . . *Haughtiness*!

Huh?

Proverbs 6:16–19 states:

"There are six things the Lord hates, seven that are detestable to him:

- haughty eyes,
- a lying tongue,
- hands that shed innocent blood,
- a heart that devises wicked schemes,
- feet that are quick to rush into evil,
- a false witness who pours out lies,
- and a man who stirs up dissension among brothers."

Stunned by the implication of this verse, I ran to the dictionary for a definition:

haughty (adj.): "Proud and vain to the point of arrogance."

Hmmm. Did this description fit me? Did it fit anyone I know? Had I ever been proud or vain to the point of arrogance? Could I say "yes" to any of the following questions?

- Had I ever treated the guy who bags my groceries like the "help"?
- Had I ever flaunted my material wealth to those with less . . . my jewelry, cars, clothes?
- Had I ever put someone down by bragging about myself?

- Do I judge people on the basis of money and power and use the material focus as a barometer to influence how I treat them?
- Am I cruel, dismissive, or intolerant to people who don't agree with me?
- Do I pick my friends on the basis of what their homes look like or their income levels?
- Am I afraid to get too close to people who look indigent and from the other side of the tracks?
- Are there things that are beneath me, such as serving others and cleaning?
- Had I ever been secretly pleased about the downfall or misfortune of someone who's better looking, smarter, or wealthier than me?

What a jolt this self-examination was to my life. Whoa! It would ultimately shape my view of others. Was I ready for it?

The Bible tells us that God hates haughtiness. Not that He has an aversion to it. Not that He finds it offensive. He *hates* it. Wow! This prominent headlining of a human condition that I sometimes find annoying (but not criminal) suggests to me that I don't have to do extreme things like murder to extremely displease our God. Would I ever put a snob and a killer in the same bucket? Probably not! Well, guess what? God just might!

This brought me face-to-face with some serious questions. Was I rationalizing the little ways in which I erred? Was I underestimating the severity with which God views my transgressions? Was I looking at the Ten Commandments and saying, "I'm seven out of ten. I'm good!" Even if I was nine out of ten and still "haughty," I was in trouble. Maybe life's "little sins" like haughtiness were bigger than I knew. Maybe . . . there's no such thing as a little sin.

The book of Genesis puts it like this: "sin is crouching at your door; it desires to have you, but you must master it" (Genesis 4:7).

Many of us step into sin's path every day of our lives. The traps of so-called "little sins" don't have red horns or yellow fangs or go bump in the night. They are more like small potholes in the road. Sometimes we drive over a dip and feel a bit of a jolt. Other times we don't feel a thing. But if we plow over enough little holes in the road our front end will be out of alignment, our tires will be badly worn, and we'll be headed for an unexpected tour of a ditch.

So it is with the little sins. Our earthly self may be cruising through life committing sin after sin after sin, but our body and mind are totally oblivious. Our soul, though, knows the score.

Sin has a tendency to blind us. Even though God laid down a clear and direct code of conduct in the Ten Commandments, layers below the surface of those commandments are the smaller nuances of sin which creep quietly and insidiously into our lives. They make small, daily skid marks. What do these little sins look like?

- Have we ever bought something solely for the purpose of showing it off?
- Have we ever "slightly" exaggerated our charitable gifts at tax time?
- Have we ever taken home a few of our employer's office supplies . . . pens, paper clips, copy paper?
- Have we ever been a party to negative "chit chat" about someone who's not in the room?
- Have we ever zipped into the last parking space in a busy lot because we got there two seconds before the old lady creeping toward the space in the beat-up Buick?
- Have we ever left a smear of lipstick on that pretty white blouse we just tried on in the department store and then turned around and quietly put it back on the rack?
- Have we ever averted our eyes in disgust from a homeless man who's lying in the gutter?
- Have we ever been so busy that we haven't had five minutes to return a phone call from a friend in need?

- Have we ever turned someone else's problems into an opportunity to talk about ourselves?
- Have we ever said "yes" to an invitation that we knew we weren't going to keep because it was easier than saying "no"?

Yes, **little sins**—the small, almost invisible faults that silently tear down our character and our moral resiliency. *Little sins*—the blind spots that make us more vulnerable to the larger scope of evil.

Psalm 51 provides insight into the pull of sin. King David was an individual strongly blessed by the Lord. He was rife with knowledge and had a keen discernment of good and evil. Yet, he succumbed to sin when he slept with Bathsheba, a woman who was not his wife. After his passion ran its course, David was busted up emotionally. He knew he had sinned against God. He knew better than to sleep with Bathsheba, but he did it anyway. Finally, when David learned she was pregnant with his child, he schemed to have her husband murdered in battle.

In his appeal to God for forgiveness, David speaks to the inescapable human condition of sinfulness: "Surely I was sinful at birth, sinful from the time my mother conceived me" (Psalm 51:5).

It's hard to imagine a sweet little baby as a sinner, but this verse presupposes that the grip of sin is simply unavoidable.

The baby who turns into the child and then turns into an adult will sin. Sin is such a part of our earthly existence; it just is. For the person who seeks high Christian standards and a worthy walk with God, this verse feels a bit like a wet blanket in a snowstorm. It suggests to us, "How on earth do we get around this sin thing?"

There's more bad news in the book of Romans:

> I know that nothing good lives in me, that is, in my sinful nature. For I have the desire to do what is good, but I cannot carry it out. For what I do is not the good I want to do; no, the evil I do not want to do—this I keep on doing. Now if I do what I do not want to do, it is no longer I who do it, but it is sin living in me that does it (Romans 7:18–20).

How depressing! This is a verse about being swamped in sin. About having an internal autopilot that defaults to the wrong course! About having a will that wants to go in one direction and a life that veers the opposite way.

Should we as Christians throw up our hands and say, "I give up. I may be justified in Jesus Christ, but I'm just destined to keep sinning my way through this life?" Well, hang on, because hope comes flooding our way as the Scriptures speak to the powerful antidote of wisdom in Proverbs:

> Do not forsake wisdom, and she will protect you; love
> her, and she will watch over you. Wisdom is supreme;
> therefore get wisdom. Though it cost all you have, get
> understanding (Proverbs 4:6–7).

I was somewhat clueless when it came to sin. I celebrated my morality by benchmarking against the Ten Commandments. I slid a little here and a little there, but on the whole, I would tell myself: *I did all right! This month, I'm eight out of ten! Fabulous!*

Many of us have this mentality, but we're completely and totally misguided. James suggests that God does not distinguish a stumble from a fall: "For he who keeps the whole law and yet stumbles at just one point is guilty of breaking all of it" (James 2:10).

There's no big sin. No medium sin. No little sin. It's all sin. Sin is *sin*. And God abhors it!

There are seven underlying platforms of human vulnerability that account for many of the "little sins" in our lives. These platforms are at the root of many things that we do and say. They may make us feel vaguely bad, a bit naughty, or maybe we feel nothing at all.

The roots of **little sin** fall into the following areas:

- *Unfair Judgments*—how our view of surface indicators and appearances leads us to make false and harmful conclusions about others.

- *Vanity*—how focusing on our looks and worldly accomplishments propels us into an exhausting, spinning, competitive state that undermines our walk with God.
- *Materialism*—how commercialism, excess spending, and misarranging our priorities distance us from God.
- *Boredom*—how an idle, unchallenged mind feeds itself on destructive earthly nourishment like gossip and pop culture.
- *Omission*—how we "look the other way" and slip into a net of inertia when people need us the most.
- *Indolence*—how our over-scheduled, consumer-oriented lifestyle drains us of the energy required to give to those who don't have the means to "return the favor."
- *Broken Promises and Empty Words*—how our spiritual and earthly relationships suffer when we don't keep our commitments and mean what we say.

While these weaknesses plague men and women equally, they manifest themselves differently along the lines of the sexes, particularly in the areas of vanity and boredom. While there are plenty of exceptions to the rule, vanity by and large exhibits itself differently between men and women. The focus on personal appearance and beauty, which leads to envy and competition and, at worst case, eating disorders, is a predominantly female issue. Men's vanity is far more likely to manifest itself in the area of sports and the workplace. In terms of boredom, the inclination to gossip or shop till you drop is also much more of a female thing. Men are far more likely to fall into boredom traps involving things like sports addictions, alcohol and drug abuse, and pornography. (Later we will see that pornography is not just a guy issue.)

In the following chapters, we will look closely at these seven platforms of sin as they relate to women. We will conclude our walk through the "little sins" with a plan for waging battle against the grassroots evil in our lives that distances us from God.

Looks Can Be Deceiving: The Sin of Unfair Judgments

4

ONE OF MY favorite gauzy memories from childhood was born in a field of soft green grass near our home in Springfield, Virginia. It was there that I used to watch clouds slowly morph in the sky overhead. I remember the mild blue days of early fall and watching as splotches of shapeless clouds became clowns and angels and butterflies before melting back into simple ribbons of white. From underneath the lithe and wavy branches of a willow tree, I recall looking up and pondering the brain-bending and elusive prospect of infinity. It just blew my mind to imagine that God's great sky goes on and on and on.

Cloud watching in the great outdoors was a wonderfully peaceful and meditative experience my Texas-raised children will never know because of one indomitable little menace— the fire ant. Reclining in grass is not the smartest way to pass time in these parts because . . . fire ants rule.

A fire ant is a tiny creature that packs a walloping punch. For much of the year, telltale heaps of brick-red dirt pellets pointing to the tip of the ants' subterranean home are every few feet in many grassy areas of Texas. The fire ant is a hostile, easily agitated Type A pest. It's also part of a rigidly knit clan that lives and breathes to serve its queen and protect her eggs. When a fire ant senses danger, it secretes pheromones that can be smelled and then emitted by other ants. Once this scent invades the air, the ants mobilize with a ferocious and focused agenda to defend and attack. An encounter with one of these little titans will linger in the mind long after the "ouch" is gone.

Now, perception versus reality in the ant's world is not always one in the same. Fire ants don't need a real threat to go nuclear. I could be walking by with no intent to trod anywhere near their home. Or someone could have just tossed a banana peel on the sidewalk near a mound. The ant does not stop to analyze the potentiality of the threat. It perceives danger, emits a battle cry, and rallies the troops in a declaration of war.

God has given humans a far more sophisticated armament of tools to aid perception. The five senses—seeing, hearing, touching, tasting, and smelling—allow us to take in the scope of our environment and process our thoughts around what we believe to be true. Before there are known facts, there are often perceptions. And these perceptions can become the basis of our final judgments, right or wrong.

The human machinery that allows us to perceive is a blessed gift from God. It makes us multidimensional thinking creatures and affords us complex, interesting lives.

But when we close the door on the possibility that our perceptions might be wrong, we enter into a realm of judgment that the Bible warns us about in the book of John: "Stop judging by mere appearances, and make a right judgment" (John 7:24).

While we're smarter than the fire ant, we also tend to react before we have the facts. This can lead us to form conclusions and opinions that are wrong. How often do we find ourselves making judgments about others based upon something that seems factual and important, but in reality has no bearing on the real nature of someone's heart or mind?

When we moved to Texas, we began attending Fellowship Church, a growing, contemporary church that draws some fifteen thousand attendees from all over the Dallas/Fort Worth area. Shortly after we joined, Todd was approached about participating in a class for new believers. While he felt that he had a solid Christian grounding, he decided to attend the class to further strengthen his ability to share his faith.

He came home from his first meeting and told me all about it. It was an interesting group, he said. There were people at different stages of life and stations of faith. He told me about one couple. The woman, he said, seemed tuned-in and engaged. Her husband had a different kind of presence. He was more reserved and hard to read on the surface.

Then it came time for Evan to talk. "What came out of his mouth," said Todd, "was this genuine flow of emotion about his faith and the importance of Christ in his life."

"He said he was 'on fire' for Jesus," Todd continued. "He's a person who will probably lead dozens of people to the Lord."

When Todd was forming his first impression, he didn't have access to Evan's inner state. He didn't have a blueprint or a map of what this fellow was all about. Only God knows what goes on in the heart of a person. In the book of Samuel, we observe that God and human beings are, not surprisingly, on different frequencies when it comes to forming opinions. Since we aren't omniscient like God, we rely more than we should on how things look.

The prophet Samuel came to understand this. God tells Samuel that he has rejected Saul as king of Israel and that he, Samuel, is to proclaim a replacement that God has already chosen. God tells Samuel that the future king is one of the eight sons of Jesse. In Bethlehem, Jesse gathers together seven of the sons so Samuel can attempt to discern who has been given the nod. Samuel is immediately drawn to Eliab: "Surely the Lord's anointed stands here before the Lord" (1 Samuel 16:6). Samuel would soon learn differently:

> But the Lord said to Samuel, "Do not consider his appearance or his height, for I have rejected him. The Lord does not look at the things man looks at. Man looks at the outward appearance, but the Lord looks at the heart" (1 Samuel 16:7).

The Bible tells us it's our natural human inclination to rely upon appearances to form our opinions. Samuel saw Eliab and made a judgment about his leadership qualities based upon the way he looked. For some reason, Eliab stood apart from his brothers. Maybe he was tall. Perhaps he was muscular and handsome. It could be that he looked mature, but we learn from the Bible that Eliab's looks had no bearing on God's judgment. God had someone else in mind—Jesse's youngest son, David. The Lord didn't send Samuel on the hunt for someone who looked like Ben Hur. It was David's heart that moved the Lord.

In the absence of this all-knowing, divine insight, human beings have only perceptions to rely upon to help form opinions. Perceptions are indeed a helpful tool so long as we allow for the possibility that they can be wrong.

Before allowing our feelings about others to be written in stone, there's a simple question that we must ask ourselves before mentally closing the book on someone we don't truly know: "What are the facts?"

Webster's defines a fact as "something that has been objectively verified." A fact is not a guess, a hunch, or a gut feeling. A fact is something real and quantifiable. A fact is the truth. In my early days as a reporter, I learned a lot about the importance of laying out the facts. If I were loose or careless with the truth, I could ruin my professional reputation. I could also get sued. In both our work and day-to-day lives, *facts are important*. Yet in practice, we don't always carefully distinguish between what's real and what simply appears to be real.

We were at church one night and happened to sit next to a very pleasant, outgoing couple. She had beautifully manicured red fingernails with lots of gold and diamond jewelry on her fingers and wrists. The man had lots of jewelry too—a nice watch, a bracelet, a necklace, and a couple of rings. I noticed his wedding band was studded with diamonds. It's not that often that I see a man with a diamond wedding ring, so I did a triple take.

After the service I said to Todd, "Those people were well off, don't you think?"

"I have no idea," he said.

"Well, did you see all of their jewelry?"

"I think I noticed some of it," Todd replied.

"Come on!" I said, "They could open a counter at Tiffany's between them! You don't think they were well off?"

"I don't know," Todd replied. "Maybe they're deeply in debt."

Hmmm. Maybe they're in debt . . .

The thought that this couple might be in debt never occurred to me. I saw some sparkling jewelry and immediately concluded they were wealthy people. Maybe they were rich. Then again, maybe they were poor. Maybe they spent their life's savings on jewelry. Perhaps they didn't have a penny in the bank. Maybe the diamonds weren't real. Perhaps it was cubic zirconium twinkling. Maybe the jewelry was a gift. Perhaps someone's great aunt died and left these poor people with a rich person's diamond stash.

The point is . . . who knows? Until I see a statement from their bank, I won't know if they are rich or poor. It's pointless, I concluded, and a waste of good energy to poke around at conclusions without substantiating facts. What's worse, we find ourselves going down the wrong path by envying people or shutting doors on others based upon an incomplete or downright false set of information.

If I could just *rewind* for a moment and come at this church encounter a little differently with a focus on the facts:

We were at church one night and happened to sit next to a very pleasant, outgoing couple. She had beautifully manicured red fingernails with lots of gold and diamond jewelry on her fingers and wrists. The man had lots of jewelry too—a nice watch, a bracelet, a necklace, and a couple of rings. I noticed his wedding band was studded with diamonds. It's not that often that I see a man with a diamond wedding ring, so I did a triple take. I'm tempted by basic human nature to make a judgment about these people.

Before I go back to the story, I asked myself: *"What are the facts?"* What I came away with were these truths:

Here is a man and woman who appear to be friendly and happen to be wearing jewelry that looks expensive. Period.

Those are the facts. I don't know if they are wealthy or poor, shallow or deep, happy or sad, good or bad. I only know from the facts that they are, at a particular moment in time:

1) friendly,
2) wearing jewelry that looks expensive.

This alone tells me next to nothing about these people.

Looking back at many people I've met in my life, I have to wonder how many of my judgments have been wrong. Just because someone appears a certain way doesn't mean he or she *is* that way.

I know that unfair judgments have been made about me. I had an encounter with a waitress in a restaurant once that made me wonder what on earth I'd done to deserve what she dished up.

We had just flown to San Francisco . . . the five of us . . . and were driving north in a rented minivan to see my oldest brother John who lives in Oregon. John had been diagnosed with cancer and we were anxious to spend some time with him and his family. I was worried about his condition and how we would find him. I was also determined to make this trip a positive one that would allow us to celebrate the precious time spent together.

Along the way, we stopped at a pretty mountain spot in California. It was approaching dinnertime, and we came across a friendly looking little diner. The sign out front said "Family Dining," so we figured this was a good place for us.

Once inside, we waited patiently to be seated at a booth. The boys were on their very best behavior. When we took our seats, I looked over toward the kitchen and noticed a very attractive waitress talking to the cooks. She was probably in her mid-forties and had beautiful, thick, shoulder-length, blonde hair. I thought to myself, *I sure wish I had her hair*. I'd gotten a short haircut after Daniel was born and spent the next year and a half alternately growing it out and getting it all cut off again. Right before our trip, I'd gotten yet another short cut and was feeling a bit like me on the inside and someone's little brother on the outside. I imagined that this lovely waitress had never had a bad hair day! At some point she looked over at us. I gave her a big smile.

We were given ample time to look over the menu and make our selections. But our waitress, the woman with the great hair, was not reading the "closed menu, we're ready to order" cues. We waited and waited and waited. She took orders from everyone around us. She helped clear away people's dirty dishes. When she'd done all of that, she went back behind the counter, leaned against a wall, and leisurely sipped a soda. Todd had to eventually get up and go over to her to ask if she'd come to our table. Maybe she didn't realize we were in her section, I rationalized. We continued to be very pleasant to her and treated her, as we always try to treat others, with respect and warmth. As she was taking our order, I noticed she wasn't forthcoming about things like "What's your soup of the day?" She muttered that she'd have to check. She never afforded us direct eye contact and acted like it was a big imposition to wait on us. I decided to pass on the soup so as not to further irritate her. We placed our order and she walked away.

"She must be having a bad day," Todd whispered.

"I should say so," I replied.

Then, I took note how her bad day was affecting the other customers around us. To my surprise, she was cheerful, smiling, and eager to serve everyone else. What was it about us? The boys were coloring with crayons on the throwaway menus and quietly amusing themselves. We had been courteous and warm. What gave here?

After our order had been placed, we waited a half hour or more for the food to come out. By now, the kids were getting hungry and starting to squirm. I looked toward the kitchen and saw plates of food sitting under hot lights on the counter ready to be delivered. It looked to me as if it might be our order. *Oh good*, I thought. *It will be out before the boys start chewing on their feet!* Our waitress passed the plates on the counter a few times as she casually sipped on that soda. After a few minutes, I tried to motion her over to inquire about getting some crackers or bread for the children if it was going to be much longer. She just ignored me. Todd tried to get her attention. She ignored him.

Now, our good cheer was fading fast. We were hungry. And we were blatantly being "dissed" by our waitress. I was ready to get out of my chair to get some action, but before I could, she grabbed the plates and started heading our way. Then she just sort of dumped the food in front of us and walked away. No "Have a nice dinner!" No "Can I get you some more water?" No nothing!

Getting the check was the final insult. Our meals had been long finished, but the waitress with the lovely hair had no interest in clearing our tables or in handing over a bill. By now, Daniel was crying loudly and Colin and John were begging to leave. Todd took Daniel out into the parking lot so we wouldn't upset the other customers. I tried, to no avail, to get the waitress to bring us our check. She passed by repeatedly within a few feet of us as I said, "Excuse me, please." But she just walked on by. This happened three times before I finally shot out of my chair, grabbed John and Colin, and made a beeline to the front of the restaurant where I begged the hostess to help us settle the bill and get us out of there. I was so upset I was shaking.

"For the first time in my life," I said to Todd, as we walked toward our car, "I have a small sense of what it must have felt like to be a minority in America in the 1950s."

For whatever reason, this woman just did not like the way we looked. I've always sympathized with the plight of minorities and imagined I understood the sting of discrimination. Until I experienced this kind of prejudice firsthand—what it felt like to be judged and mistreated on the basis of surface-level qualities that don't begin to get at who I am—I had no idea how deep it cuts. Prejudice hurts. It has no basis in fact. Prejudice is about perception gone bad. It's haughtiness with flying colors.

A book published in 1996 blew the lid off some common perceptions about rich people. *The Millionaire Next Door,* by

Thomas J. Stanley and William D. Danko, takes a walk through the lives of America's self-made elite. And what we learn from this book is that rich people don't always look and act like J. R. Ewing! They are a surprisingly normal, budget-conscious group. Self-made millionaires are more likely to have a charge card for Sears than Neiman Marcus. They aren't cruising around in Bentleys; they drive pick-up trucks. Millionaires budget for household items; their wives clip coupons. So the "would you pass me some Grey Poupon" perception we have of wealthy people turns out to be more fantasy than reality. Most self-made millionaires in America are people living very unpretentious lives. They are individuals who exercise wisdom by living below rather than beyond their means.

Many of us aspire to have the appearance of wealth, yet we're in essence chasing an earthly illusion, because the people we want to look like don't always look the way we think they should.

My friend Helen recounts a story about "Aunt Ethel" and "Uncle Roger," who owned a ranch in Oklahoma. As a child, Helen visited them every Thanksgiving. She has fond memories of playing in the dusty old red barn and tinkling the badly, out-of-tune ivories of a well-worn upright piano. Uncle Roger, she says, was a very simple man.

"He was a gentle, sweet person," Helen said. "Uncle Roger was very stereotypical in a lot of ways. If you ran into him in the grocery store, you'd just know he worked outdoors ten hours a day. He'd be wearing a pair of faded overalls with a red handkerchief hanging out of his back pocket. He had a worker's hands and a very humble demeanor."

Imagine the family's shock when Uncle Roger died and left Aunt Ethel with millions of dollars in the bank.

"Uncle Roger was a multi-millionaire," Helen said. "He was wildly rich and no one knew."

So, as the old adage goes: "appearances can be deceiving." Before we leap to conclusions about people based upon surface-level indicators, we should hold on to our judgments until we know the facts. Even though we don't have the benefit of God's all-knowing insight into each other's hearts and minds, that doesn't mean we're without tools to help us make better judgments. The Bible makes reference upon reference to God's view of our conduct when it comes to how He will judge us. This is a good barometer for all of us. Beyond how a person looks or what comes out of her mouth, what about the actions? How does she conduct herself? Does she lift up those around her? What are the products or fruits of her life's work? Are these things rooted in Christian faith or motivated by self-interest? Use the Apostle John's words as a rule of thumb: "Dear children, let us not love with words or tongue but with actions and in truth. . . . For God is greater than our hearts, and he knows everything" (1 John 3:18, 20).

Reflections on Judgments

- Was there ever a time you formed an opinion about someone that turned out to be false?
- What were the outward qualities or behaviors associated with this person that led you to judge him/her unfairly?
- What were the facts that changed your opinion?
- Is there someone in your life today you may be judging unfairly? Who is he/she?
- Could you be wrong about what's causing him/her to act or appear a certain way? What are some other possible explanations for his/her behavior?

It's a Vain, Vain World: The Sin of Vanity

5

WHEN WE MOVED to Texas from Virginia, I was eight months pregnant with our third child. I'd lived on the East Coast most of my life. My parents and friends were there. It's where I'd planted roots. But my husband's career was propelling us across the country. I'd quit working outside the home a couple years earlier and was now a full-time mom to two toddlers and one-in-waiting. Though it couldn't have come at a more inconvenient time for us, I tried to put the move in a positive light. It was a promotion for my husband, and he was excited. The boys were so young they were pretty much unfazed by the prospects of striking camp and going west.

I was at an advanced stage in the pregnancy and showing some signs that Junior might come early. So time was of the essence. Once the job offer was formally extended, we needed to move quickly in order to get ourselves ready for the baby's arrival on the other end. When the offer came, we bagged some essentials and hopped a plane for Dallas. As we climbed into the sky, my knuckles knotted white around a damp, wadded up tissue I'd used to mop up the tears from streaky cheeks as I waved a final good-bye to Mom and Dad from the backseat of an airport-bound taxi. In the other hand, I clung to a vial of anti-contraction drugs my doctor had prescribed . . . just in case. And that was it. We were way up high and moving quickly out of the blue and into the clouds.

I told myself when my swollen feet hit Texas soil that I would view this crazy, lightning-paced move as a great adventure. We would simply make the best of any potential crises and rely on our faith and each other to get through whatever came our way.

The spirit of adventure sustained me through a surprisingly easy delivery and an unbelievably smooth move into a new home with a new baby. God had truly paved the way for us. Still, I had no friends in Texas. We were on our own. Before long, the high of the adventure began to descend and I started to feel isolated and lonely.

We hired a mother's helper, Cindy, to get us through the first few months in the new world. She helped entertain the older boys, ages three and eighteen months, while I tried to establish a rhythm with the new baby and get my bearings in the new environment. Over the course of several weeks, we gradually fell into a routine. Soon I found enough courage to pack my brood into the car and venture out.

I had gained a lot of weight with each of my pregnancies and was still carrying about thirty extra pounds on my bone-tired body, months after the delivery. My face looked a bit like a sad moon and I hated the way I looked in pictures. I couldn't stand to pass a mirror. This affected the way I felt about virtually every aspect of my life. I was feeling pretty low. While I was never once tempted to backslide into the hellish pit of bulimia—I knew what dangers lurked there—I found myself staring down the barrel of an old and painful haunting. Once again, I was allowing the state of my appearance to set the tone for my life.

One sunny day, I loaded the boys into the car and headed to downtown Dallas to return an expensive wool sweater I'd been given as a gift. I'm allergic to wool, so I decided to treat myself to something special of my own choosing. All that extra tonnage from a let's-eat-cake pregnancy had washed my self-esteem into the gutter. This was a shopping mission that was all about bucking myself up. I loaded my three little guys in the car and we were off to one of the city's finest department stores.

As I squeezed my oversized double stroller through the door and stepped foot inside the store, I felt immediately ill at ease. Everyone I passed seemed so beautifully put together. The shoppers were dressed to kill in designer clothes and big chunky jewelry. Almost everyone was blonde and thin as a weed. In contrast, I had three small children in tow and was wearing my postpartum uniform of elastic-waist shorts and an oversized T-shirt that covered the ripples and rolls of new motherhood. The older boys were in the stroller and I was wearing the baby in one of those earth-mother slings. I defined frump. Many of the stylish shoppers that day looked at me as if I'd missed the turn to the dollar store. I was terribly self-conscious and feeling so small I wanted to cry. I also wanted to hoist a sign that said: "Hey, I used to be somebody!"

There I was, clutching my return in one hand while trying to navigate a clunky stroller and bouncing baby past these visions of beauty. I didn't even get to the casual clothes section before I spotted an expensive designer rack. The goddesses around me suddenly faded to black as I spied the most beautiful white skirt I'd ever seen. I just had to touch it. The fabric felt like soft butter and it seemed to flow even as it hung from the hanger. I had a closet full of nice clothes I used to wear to work. They hadn't been so much as looked at in years. But somehow, I felt I needed this skirt. I really needed it. I took a bit of a breath and looked at the price tag: $525.00. Whoa! I'd never spent that kind of money on one piece of an outfit. But this was different. I needed this. This would complete me. This would put me in the same league with the women I was shuffling past who were looking at me like I was some kind of bag lady. *This would show them!*

I didn't buy the skirt that day. I went home and thought about it . . . and thought about it. I was thinking about those stunning shoppers too. Boy, I sure did want to move into their league. A couple days later, I put on my maternity stretch shorts, the only thing in my closet that fit, and headed back to the store to close the deal. I felt like a million bucks walking out of that showroom with my prize. Now, I was somebody. Let there be no doubt about that! I could throw my credit card around! I could buy expensive things. I could look good. I still had it!

On the way home, I ran through the scenarios where I would wear my prize. Three children under the age of four and round-the-clock breastfeeding did not make for an easy night on the town. Wearing it around the house was out. It would be smeared with cooked carrots and orange drool before noon. And who would see me? Isn't that 99 percent of the designer clothing scene? Having the skirt is meaningless if I can't be seen and admired wearing it. So my prize hung in the closet. I passed it every day on the way to retrieve a pair of stretch pants for the real world. Still I was so pleased with my purchase. Having it just made me feel good.

About six weeks later, I found myself back at the mall where I'd made my gilded purchase. I was curious to see what was going on in the designer section, so I returned to the rack where I'd spotted the crown jewel. My jaw nearly fell off my face when I saw not one, not two, but three identical white skirts on the rack. Marked down not once, not twice, but three times! My $525.00 skirt was now selling for $66.00.

My feelings of wealth and glamour and attractiveness went to the bargain basement with it. Now I was the not-so-proud owner of a skirt no one else valued enough to buy at full price. Even at a discount, it still didn't seem to be moving.

I still have that skirt. And every time I look at it, I'm reminded of the dwindling value of things and how fleeting is the joy we take from them.

It's the same thing with new cars, isn't it? We drive that late model car off the lot and we're feeling about three planets beyond the moon superior to the people next door. But it doesn't take long for the new car smell to fade. Our three-year-old spills grape juice all over the backseat. Our teenager gets a wad of gum glued to the floor mats. Our husband dribbles his mocha latte on the console. The sparkly paint will start to dull. And that exhilarating high we felt when we first wheeled past our neighbors in that fancy new car—a high born out of vanity—goes as quickly as it came. Now the new car is just a tool that gets us from place to place . . . and we're still paying it off.

So, we are on to the next thing. On and on it goes.

Many of us are so caught up in the worldly game of adding to our possessions to fill the spiritual void in our souls. Not surprisingly, these things never complete us. Look at King Solomon, a man who found favor from God—a man blessed with unimaginable riches, bounty, and power. This was a man who was actually visited by God. King Solomon was a man who had it all and lost it when the vanities of the world became more important to him than the God Who made it all possible.

> As Solomon grew old, his wives turned his heart after other gods, and his heart was not fully devoted to the Lord, his God . . . So Solomon did evil in the eyes of the Lord (1 Kings 11:4, 6).

Solomon caved into the temptations of the flesh. He became an amasser of things. He became a mass consumer of women. He became so powerful and so ensconced in his trappings that he outgrew his need for God. He became "god." The result: he was punished for this arrogance.

> The Lord became angry with Solomon because his heart
> had turned away from the Lord, the God of Israel . . . So
> the Lord said to Solomon, "Since this is your attitude
> and you have not kept my covenant and my decrees,
> which I commanded you, I will most certainly tear the
> kingdom away from you and give it to one of your sub-
> ordinates" (1 Kings 11:9, 11).

Yes, God caused conflict and strife to rain upon Solomon's
golden world. He even cut short the blessings extended to
his children. By all accounts, we can assume that Solomon
died with an emptiness and regret in his heart. He had gotten off the main highway and found himself headed in the
wrong direction on a secondary road. His God-inspired
world careened into the material world . . . and the material
world won out.

The story of King Solomon is about the sin of vanity—
the totally egocentric focus on earthly self. It's our appearance, our accomplishments, our never-ending need to
acquire more things that the arbiters and trendsetters of the
world value. In Solomon's day, it was gold, sheep, and one's
land holdings. While gold and real estate still glitter today,
the modern vanity trap has a lot more arms and legs. In
today's world, vanity also extends to the "in" things and the

"in" people we read about in all the popular magazines. Vanity propels us to the makeup counter as we look in vain, literally, for hope in a jar. It drives us to the plastic surgeon. It makes designer clothes a must-have. Vanity parks expensive cars in our driveway. It takes us to the "in" places. And it makes puffy, prideful words fly out of our mouths about the extraordinary achievements we have personally accomplished and the laurels hanging around the heads of our family members.

Vanity makes us tireless, competitive creatures. Whether we're in someone's face with our puffery or we're a bit more sneaky with our methods of impressing people, we're like hamsters on a wheel going around and around trying to elevate ourselves to higher and higher levels on the social or economic ladder. But does the hamster ever stay atop the wheel for long? No, she goes up, goes down, and goes round and round and round.

As it relates to women and competition, the hamster on the wheel is the perfect visual for the spinning, spiraling competitive state in which we constantly find ourselves . . . whether we know it or not. Here's how it can play out in our lives:

(Ring! Ring! Mary Jane's giving her "best friend" Sally Ann a jingle.)

Mary Jane: Hi! I just got back from K-Mart. I picked up the cutest little pair of shorts.

Sally Ann: (*the subtle put-down*) Really! That's great. Actually, I was at Nordstrom's last week and picked up a few things for myself. I just love *that* store!

Mary Jane: (*on the defensive*) Oh, well, I usually shop at Nordstrom's too. I was just buying some paper towels at K-Mart and I . . .

Sally Ann: (*a stronger put-down*) You can get a great deal on the paper products at places like K-Mart. But the clothes . . . well, I prefer Nordstrom's.

Mary Jane: (*feeling competitive*) Oh, I know what you mean. And Saks. Even better.

Sally Ann: (*feeling competitive*) I love Saks! I'm there every other week. You know me, I get around!! Shop, shop, shop!

Mary Jane: (*Laughs. But inside she's feeling not so good about her K-Mart purchase. And this affects the way she feels about herself. She's also feeling distanced and out of sync with Sally Ann.*)

This is the type of conversation that transpires to varying degrees between women a lot of the time! Maybe it's about clothes. Maybe it's about jewelry. Maybe it's about how smart or athletic the kids are. Maybe it's about how great we're doing on the job. Maybe it's about how much money our husbands earn. Maybe it's about the nice places we vacation. On its surface, it's just chatty girl talk. But go a layer deeper and we'll find the seeds of competition and vanity. Does it sound familiar?

The Bible talks about the act of competition: "Each one should test his own actions. Then he can take pride in himself, without comparing himself to somebody else, for each one should carry his own load" (Galatians 6:4, 5).

Vanity-driven competition can be an all-consuming and utterly destructive force in our lives. When we find ourselves in the company of people who are constantly trying to show us how superior they are, do we jump in the game and spar with them? If so, we are fueling a poisonous pursuit. There's a principle in Psychology 101 that suggests people with brittle or weak self-esteem will build themselves up by tearing others down. It's a human relation tactic that's as old as the hills. As it relates to the day-to-day interactions between women, it's not always an aggressive, blatant, or flashy maneuver. It can be subtle and tricky. It's the lady friend who asks about our daughter so she can brag about her son. It's mind games. And it's dangerous.

The vanity trap for women is often wedged in things that relate to the way we look and the things we wear. At first, vanity can give us a good feeling. There's something viscerally pleasing about fitting in and rising above. We spot a shoe trend among the rich and celebrated in our favorite magazine. We get the shoes . . . then we're it, girl! We put on a shirt with that little horse on it and we're *Town & Country!* But the next thing we know, our neighbor has the same shoes or the same shirt. Maybe her shoes and shirt are a little better. Then we're on to the next earthly point of differentiation. And it goes on and on like that.

Vanity is a bit like a hollow, rotted out nut. The shell may be nice, but there's nothing but air and decay inside. Before long, the shell's not looking so good. Look at the maturing movie stars that are hanging on with well-manicured nails to faded youth. Their faces are pulled and drawn. Their swollen lips look like Ballpark Franks. They are doing everything earthly possible to keep their biggest asset alive—their looks. Even so, these aren't the women whose posters hang on the walls in dorms and locker rooms. Men's hearts don't skip a beat when they walk into a room. The beauty of their youth is simply gone as a matter of due course. The Bible says our beauty is destined to leave us: "Charm is deceptive, and beauty is fleeting" (Proverbs 31:30). This is a wrenching thing for many of us. Society puts a premium on good looks. When our beauty starts to fade, there's a huge mourning process for most women. The best years are over for us before we reach the halfway point of our lives. If there's nothing of substance under the shell, will we go into the sunset with sadness and bitterness in our hearts? What a waste!

There's even a popular magazine that attracts millions of loyal readers called *Vanity Fair*. As the name clearly states, it's all about vanity—a publication that tracks the famous, the profane, and the hugely egocentric. There's an edgy, sexy, over-the-top, glossy sheen around every page of *Vanity Fair*. Even the ads are seductive. *Vanity Fair* takes its readers on a wade through the murky waters of fame and notoriety. And consumers just eat it up.

I used to have a love/hate relationship with my women's magazines. I bought them faithfully—*People, Us, Vanity Fair, Talk*—because I felt I was missing something if I didn't see who was doing what to whom and who was wearing this or that. I loved the entertainment value of these magazines. But I also found that I somehow felt a little worse about myself after having read them. *Darn! I'll never have Penelope Cruz's hair! I'll never have Christy Brinkley's face! I'll never have Jennifer Aniston's body! And Catherine Zeta-Jones? Uh . . . I'll never have anything she's got!* I had to come face to face with my own vanities and insecurities every time I left the supermarket with one of these magazines.

I knew from my dark days as a bulimic that it wasn't healthy for me to continue to immerse myself in the world of skinny models and fashions for size zeroes. Even so, I continued to compare myself to the beautiful people I saw in the media. When I fell short (which was always), I somehow felt a little worse about myself on the surface and beneath. I realized I would never look like Demi Moore.

But when God began revealing the presence of "little sins" in my life, a strange thing happened between my women's magazines and me. I acquired some discernment about them, as well. I no longer looked at these publications and the gorgeous women in them with a heart of envy. I stopped feeling so bad about my hair, my face, my body, and everything about me that will never look like a Hollywood starlet. Instead, I could see as clear as day the teetering, superficial lives many celebrities lead. I began to feel sadness in my heart for the lovely women I used to envy, like the movie stars who vie for headlines by seeing who can wear the least amount of clothes to the big awards ceremonies. They've climbed to the top on the virtues of their beauty or their talent as they pretend to be someone else in films. Then, the rest of their career is spent maintaining an illusion! How do they stay beautiful? How do they keep getting good movie roles? How on earth do they stay on top? Well, the sad truth is: most of them simply don't. The former beauties make way for the new beauties. And yesterday's great actresses tend to vanish.

When I see the new "it" girl emerge every few years, I think to myself, *Wow. I hope she's working on something other than her abs, because that's not going to sustain her in this life. And it's certainly not going to get her to the next world.*

God gave us a body to care for and to nurture. Staying healthy and taking care of our body is a godly thing. The Bible talks at various points about the perils of excess and the virtues of healthy living. Physical health and vitality is an enabler of good works. If God had not enabled me to overcome bulimia and restore my mind and body to health, I would probably be dead right now. Keeping fit is a worthy, God-directed aspect of honoring the Lord. But when the focus of our life is how fat are my thighs, how gray is my hair, how expensive are my clothes, and how do I look in a bikini, they become a blinding distraction from the real order of business—getting closer to God and growing spiritually.

In reality, God doesn't care about any of that stuff. He could care less whether we're having a good hair day or a bad hair day. He's tuned into our hearts. He wants our souls. And, as far as I know, a soul isn't the least bit concerned about wrinkles, dimples on our thighs, or flyaway hair.

I continued to subscribe to a variety of entertainment magazines and read them faithfully for many months after it occurred to me that this wasn't the most nourishing entertainment. Something about the world of high fashion and celebrity gossip just continued to reel me in. Over time I did begin to notice that my sensitization to the shadowy side of today's media began to take away the pleasure I derived from curling up on the sofa with many of these magazines, particularly the ones that plumbed the seedy depths of fame. It came to the point where I could take them or leave them. One night I knew I'd read my last issue of one magazine in particular. For the better part of two hours, I had immersed myself in stories peppered with "f" and "s" words about murder, rape, and homosexuality. My eyes had taken in countless advertisements depicting nudity, sadomasochism, and blatant exploitation of young women and men. When I shut the cover on this magazine, I felt like a toxic waste dump. I had just fed myself with garbage and was sitting on my couch steeping in filth. My love affair with the dark side of celebrity was over.

Granted, the material world is the world in which we live. As such, it's hard to divorce ourselves from the never-ending quest for more material things. Given a choice of living in a slum or a nice suburban neighborhood, there are few who would reach Mother Teresa's level of self-sacrifice. Still, is it possible to live in the world and not be consumed, enslaved, and embittered by it?

The Bible points out that we are inherently vain: "The Lord knoweth the thoughts of man, that they are vanity" (Psalm 94:11 KJV).

It also warns about the blinding nature of our vanities: "For in his own eyes he flatters himself too much to detect or hate his sin" (Psalm 36:2).

It's a fundamental flaw in our human makeup, but do we have to descend into a state of ruin like Solomon? Or can we get ourselves to an enlightened place and become sensitized to the dangers of living to glorify our appearance and our earthly accomplishments?

Validate Our Impulses

The key to getting out of the trap is to look vanity in the eye. Learn to recognize it. Discern the difference between real needs and perceived needs or more aptly, needs versus wants. *Validate our impulses.* As we've seen, the Bible tells us that our human nature makes us intrinsically vain. As such, our impulses and actions are set on a default that makes us susceptible to vanity's trappings. Adopt a mindset that takes a *time-out* before making the big purchases, flaunting something earthly, or saying boastful things.

When we're in this *time-out* mode, we must take stock of our real needs and determine what our actions will do to satisfy those needs. Are we buying that new car for the cargo space? Or do we want to show it off? Are we purchasing that new dress because our wardrobe could use a boost? Or are we trying to upstage coworker, Jenny, at the office party? What's the real deal? If we search our soul and come up with "show it off" or "dust Jenny," our motives are purely vain. We're trying to buy ourselves out of a state of emptiness—a state that only God can permanently deliver us from.

Vanity splintered my relationship with Cindy, the mother's helper we hired when we first moved to Texas. Cindy was great with the kids. We had a good relationship, a friendship relationship. We laughed our way through much of the day. Cindy told me she loved being with us. We loved being with her. I paid her $9.00 an hour, which was the fee requested for Cindy on behalf of her agency.

We were in the car coming home from the grocery store one day. I'd just had a baby and was feeling about as attractive as a wildebeest. As a full-time mom, I hadn't had a performance review or a raise in a good long while, so I was especially vulnerable to the vanity trap. We were driving down the road, and I began bragging about how much money I earned as a consultant after leaving the workforce of a large corporation. I expressed myself in terms of my hourly rate, which was nearly twenty times hers. Cindy audibly took in some air and remained unusually quiet for the rest of the ride home. In less than one minute's time, I had turned a friendly, egalitarian relationship into a vain competition over money. Everything had changed. Now we weren't simply a mother and her wonderful assistant, we were *more money* versus *less money*. I opened my mouth and spat out a vanity, and I paid dearly. Our relationship never recovered. A few days later she came to me and asked for a healthy raise. There was a new undercurrent of friction in our relationship. It was obvious to me that she was now uncomfortable with my perceived wealth, despite the fact I no longer earned a dime. My family lost her over this . . . and it was all because of my vanity. So validate your impulses! Think before you talk! Think before you act! Take a time-out!

Move On

Another way to overcome vanity is to *move on*. We must grow into new stages of our lives and leave the past in the past. If we're forty years old and competing with our eighteen-year-old self, it's time to *move on*. It's the proverbial "mid-life crisis." But for some of us, the crisis never ends, because we may have allowed ourselves to be defined by this ghost—that point at which we were most physically attractive.

I saw a comedy many years ago about the zany exploits of an aging rock band struggling to keep alive the bloom and energy of its youth. This movie took a satirical look at what happens when people fail to move on. These past-primetime characters tried to cope with the loss of a panting, young fan base and the reality of bad, middle-age hair days. In real life, it's not so comical when our world is oriented around youth and we're no longer young.

As I mature, I try to make peace with the fact that the outside me is inevitably changing. There were points in my life when this caused me great fear and concern. I had allowed myself to be defined by secular society's definition of beauty. Yet, as I grow in my relationship with Christ, I gain a deepening sense of acceptance and peace with what's in store for my earthly body as I mature. When I'm seventy years old, I won't look like I did when I was thirty. No amount of cosmetic surgery or makeup artistry will return the pure state of my youth. I have to be ready to move on! I believe it's wise to start today preparing for that day. We need to develop interests, dimensions, and depth that will transition us gracefully into new phases of our lives.

Ann Hardy, a grandmother of five, is a Texas artist who epitomizes true beauty through her outlook and zealous pursuit of personal growth. Her dreamy impressionistic paintings, which have been exhibited and sold throughout the world, are just one creative spectrum of an earthly life that's dynamic, robust, and continually evolving.

"You must live life fully and well," Ann told me, "and a big part of that is being at home in your own skin."

Ann doesn't entertain the thought of idling in park while the world speeds past. If there's an opportunity to learn and grow, she's going for the checkered flag. Over the years, Ann took a twenty-year-old mule around Texas following the Sesquicentennial Wagon Train. She hired on as a cook aboard a fifty-one-foot sailboat in the Grenadines. She backpacked solo on thirty dollars a day through Scotland and England. She drove eight women on a painting escape through potentially dangerous terrain in Guatemala. She signed on with Habitat for Humanity in Belize. She camped out under the stars in the Rocky Mountains, Mexico, and Italy.

As I reflected upon all the gusto that Ann Hardy has grabbed out of life, I realized what great stories she must have tucked away in the rich reserves of her memory. I wondered what tales are still to come from a mind and body that is continually moving on in exciting and meaningful ways.

I also reflected upon those who transition into mature stages of life with a different perspective. Sadly, there are some whose main obsession as they grow older is that fading rearview image of youth that leads them to extreme cosmetic surgery and other drastic measures designed to fool Mother Nature.

The book of Ecclesiastes tells us there are distinct phases in life: "There is a time for everything, and a season for every activity under heaven" (Ecclesiastes 3:1).

The word *season* gives us a simple but powerful mental image. As human beings, we truly have a seasonal dimension to our earthly lives. Just as we wouldn't wear a T-shirt and sandals in a Minnesota winter, it's unwise to live our lives out of season. When we are in the summer or fall of our existence, that's our season. To grow and mature gracefully, we can't spend our summer pining for spring. Instead, we need to enjoy the landscape and fruits of the season in which we dwell. We need to realize that, like the fruits of the earth, we can grow infinitely better with time. We all know what summer fruit tastes like out of season. The peach in the bin at the grocery store in March may look good, but it doesn't have the flavor or substance of the fruits that are harvested when they are mature. We must celebrate our growth and cherish our inner beauty throughout all the days of our lives.

Anchor Ourselves to God

The other weapon against vanity is simply and powerfully— God Himself. *Anchor ourselves to God.* The lures of vanity are around every corner, so we need to anchor ourselves firmly to the Creator. We must depend upon His hand to keep us stable and less susceptible to temptation.

"Lead us not into temptation, but deliver us from evil." Many of us utter this petition every week at church, but do we really know what we're saying? Or are we just filling the air with some words we memorized? Pray it with purpose and passion. Call upon the comfort of the Holy Spirit to whisper and warn when temptation is afoot. Pray for the insight to discern clearly good from evil. Secular society would have us latch onto two worldly things—power for protection and money as a safeguard. But power and money do not provide stability. One day they're here; the next day they're gone. The only true and enduring stronghold is God.

If we doubt the mercurial nature of earthly sources of security, look no further than the stock market. The same financial entity that turned a cadre of computer techies into overnight millionaires with the tech-stock boom also pulled the rug out from underneath a lot of well-shod feet when the value of these enterprises began to tank in the late 1990s. The current state of the market could be described as volatile and uncertain at best. For most of us, our relative wealth, power, and prestige are totally at the mercy of the economy. Even our physical health and well-being can deteriorate in a matter of days or hours. Praise God, our eternal state of being with the Lord is not so thin and precarious!

> Turn from evil and do good; then you will dwell in the land forever. For the Lord loves the just and will not forsake his faithful ones (Psalm 37:27, 28).

Reflections on Vanity

- Are there areas in which you are vulnerable to vanities? (Example: Do you ever feel competitive with friends over who has the most expensive clothes, home furnishings, etc.?)
- Could your vanities be hurting your relationships? How?
- What are some steps you can take immediately to minimize vanity's negative impact on your life and strengthen your relationships? (Example: Broaden your dialogue with friends to include areas outside fashion and beauty and other purely superficial topics.)

The Thing Trap:
The Sin of Materialism

6

'TWAS THE NIGHT before Christmas and all was stirring in the house. The last of my three adrenaline-propelled toddlers had run out of fuel and crashed on the bedroom floor just before midnight. But the workday for Todd and me had just begun. Cranky and spent, I retreated to our bedroom closet and dragged out five fat rolls of Cookie Monster wrapping paper. For the next two hours, Todd and I lost our human form and became somber, mechanical, toy-wrapping robots.

"This is how carpal tunnel begins," I said to Todd as I yanked, tore, and plastered my sixtieth piece of tape to my twentieth toy action figure. Todd's reply was sort of dreary and unintelligible. I didn't have the energy to follow up with a "Huh?" We just went about our wrapping business in silence. By 2 A.M. on Christmas morning it was finally over. We were done wrapping for the year. We took a few bites out of the Vanilla Wafers on Santa's cookie plate, smeared some Crest on our teeth, and fell into bed.

It was an early wake-up call a few hours later. Our three-year-old was the first to arrive on the scene with a whoop and rally cry declaring Santa had come! By 6 A.M., they were all on the loose. Lying in bed listening to bombastic pounding of six little feet, I had hopes that they might open a present or two on their own and give us five more minutes of rest. I no sooner indulged that fantasy than I had three wildly flailing little boys on top of us in bed. Todd took an elbow to the eye and I nearly lost my spleen. We were dragged like tormented hostages from bed into a blurry world. I was so tired I could have been tipped over like a sleeping cow. Todd was still dreary and unintelligible. This was not what Christmas was all about. Somehow we had lost our way.

In years past, I was able to fold Jesus into all the advertising and commercial hoopla and allow the two forces to coexist in a joyous and merry convergence of spiritual and worldly celebration. But this year it was different. We had allowed commercialism to drown out Jesus. Rather than slowing down and reflecting with spiritual joy upon the birth of our Savior, we were going full tilt through a season that demanded shopping, cooking, cleaning, sending cards, wrapping presents, parties, and events that sucked the very life out of us. By Christmas morning, Todd and I were overcooked and wilted.

We all gathered around the tree that morning and helped our boys bust through the perimeter of an emporium of gifts that had spread out like wall-to-wall carpeting. Todd and I curled up on the couch and watched with mixed emotions as our bug-eyed little boys blew through toy after toy. Wrapping paper was riding the air like mini-whirlwinds as gift after gift was given a quick once-over and then shoved aside to make way for the next conquest.

"Look at all of this stuff," Todd said to me.

"It's terrible," I replied. "We've got it all wrong."

I know from talking to many families over the years that the scene at our house on that Christmas morning was not unique. Children's wish lists have grown and parents are into fulfillment. I long for protective clothing and headgear every time I enter a toy store in the days leading up to Christmas. Legions of parents are powering shopping carts through hive-like colonies of people buzzing in the aisles. These shoppers have the fervor and passion of a thirteenth-century crusade; and they're prepared to do battle over the hottest gifts. On the one hand, I feel somewhat sympathetic for the loving parent who stops at nothing to bring a twinkle to Junior's eye. On the other hand, I'm concerned about another generation of kids who have high expectations and a sense of entitlement about the material dimension of their world.

Every Christmas I'm reminded how easy it is to lose perspective and focus too much on things. One other incident put materialism into perspective for me. I was at the neighborhood pool with my children one summer morning. I had packed towels, snacks, and drinks. I had sunscreen, dry clothes, and diapers. I could have filled a footlocker with everything I needed for an hour of fun in the sun. However, on this particular day, I forgot to bring toys. So there we stood on the edge of the wading pool with nothing to delight us but ourselves and a few hundred gallons of water. The children began to groan, "You forgot the toys!"

Fortunately, it wasn't long before two other mothers with small children arrived with a load of toys. Wow! I didn't know there were that many things that could float and sink and bob in the water. Fortunately, there were more than enough playthings to share so each of my children found something they could throw or squirt. Those toys were a big hit at first, but I noticed that within five or ten minutes the children began to lose interest.

Then something interesting happened. The other mothers had just finished drinking coffee out of Styrofoam cups, and the children now had *new* pool toys! The kids used those throwaway cups to scoop water and splash one another. One child would pour water from one cup to another as the other children looked on with fascination. All the while, $150.00 worth of Grade A water toys just floated on by.

I was reminded again of that Christmas when Todd and I had stayed up half the night wrapping dozens of presents and how those gifts were ripped into and cast aside the instant something better came along. As I watched a small group of children take turns with a couple discarded foam cups, I was struck by the fact that we steal a mindset of contentment from our children when we indulge the contemporary worldview that more is better and expensive is best.

I like to picture the downside of materialism with three character types:

The Peacock

She uses things to puff herself up and cultivate an identity that masks her low self-esteem. The peacock likes expensive clothes and jewelry. She drives a late model car and likes to flaunt her financial prowess. Her zip code and upper-tier associates are important to her. She lets you know she's in the money.

Characteristics:
- Brags a lot
- Flaunts expensive clothes and accessories
- Likes to compete with other peacocks
- Listens poorly

The Junkie

She needs to acquire things to get a "feel-good" high. Instead of turning to God, she goes to Macy's. The high from a shopping fix feels real good, but she's going to come down hard and fast. When she does, she's depressed. Then she's off to Nordstrom's . . .

Characteristics:
- Shops till she drops—often!
- Prone to extreme highs and lows
- May be deeply in debt
- Often feels helpless and out of control (except when she's shopping)

The Squirrel

She is the hoarder. The nuts in her cheek are the shoes in her closet, the seventeen jars of peanut butter in her pantry, and the stuff that's spilling out of cracks and crevices all over her house. The squirrel amasses things to create an earthly cocoon of security. Clothing, accessories, and an exploding pantry help insulate her from uncertainty and fear of the unknown.

Characteristics:
- Not a cheerful giver
- Has things and backup to things (e.g., six pairs of the same shoe)
- Worries about her things (e.g., better not spill a beverage on *her* carpet!)

In the previous chapter, we looked at aspects of materialism through the lens of vanity—how the acquisition of things can be used as a tool to shape people's perceptions based upon *external* appearances. But there are other dimensions of materialism. They stem from our attempts to fill the emptiness *inside* with things that will bring instant satisfaction. When we turn to things other than God, we find that happiness is fleeting and often troublesome.

The Bible warns that the accumulation of earthly things is a misdirected pursuit: "Whoever loves money never has enough; whoever loves wealth is never satisfied with his income. This too is meaningless" (Ecclesiastes 5:10). But are we to understand that owning and acquiring things are evil?

Are we to feel guilty about having possessions? There's plenty of scriptural evidence that God indeed provides for our enjoyment.

In Proverbs, we're told: "The blessing of the Lord brings wealth, and He adds no trouble to it" (Proverbs 10:22). In Ecclesiastes, we learn: "When God gives any man wealth and possessions, and enables him to enjoy them . . . this is a gift from God" (Ecclesiastes 5:19). Clearly God doesn't look upon most things as evil. It's our relationship with things that gets us into trouble. Materialism does not speak to the object but the application—how we *use* our things.

Todd and I were at a Bible study group one evening before Christmas, the year after we had the Toys "R" Us showroom bonanza under our tree. I was expressing my frustrations about Christmas past when our friend, Jerry, shared a story that touched my heart.

"After our children had grown, we decided to do away with gifts at Christmas and put the focus back on Jesus," Jerry said.

"So after a nice dinner on Christmas, we put on little hats and go out on the front porch where we blow party horns, ring bells, and sing songs. It's our birthday party for Jesus," he said.

I heard of another family that limits Christmas gifts to three presents per child. The basis for their decision is the wise men that presented three gifts to the Christ child. These are but two ways to refocus our celebration of Christmas and downplay the thing trap. Other families have their own traditions around gift giving or special ways to headline Christ. While there's no prescription or template as to how we should mark this holy day, if something is clouding the real focus, maybe it should be rethought. If gizmos, gadgets, and earthly trappings have stolen the spotlight from the Savior, it's time to take a deep breath, slow down, and free ourselves to remember what it's all about.

This is an important point that extends beyond Christmas into every day of our lives as we take a step back and look at what we need, what we want, and where Jesus reigns in this equation.

Reflections on Materialism

- What's your most special possession? What makes it so special?
- If you could have one thing in life that's currently missing, what would it be?
- What kind of activities do you default to when you're feeling down?
- Have you ever regretted buying something? What was it and why?

- Have you ever bought a new car? How long did that new car "happy" feeling last?
- Are there things you buy for yourself that weaken you spiritually? What are they?
- What are some other activities you could engage in when you are tempted to shop for things?

Psst . . . Want to Know a Secret?: The Sin of Boredom

7

SHORTLY AFTER I graduated from college in 1983, I was hired as Director of Public Affairs for a national trade association outside Washington, D.C. I knew going into the job that it would not make me rich. My starting salary was $13,000 a year. After rent and car insurance, there wasn't much left over at the end of the month! Still, I was in love with that big title and figured it would look fabulous on my resume. Even though I was still struggling with an eating disorder, I was able to compartmentalize this problem and keep it from infiltrating and undermining the landscape of my career. After four years of college and ready to pop with great expectations, I was excited about being Ms. Director.

I was lured to the position by the headquarter executive. He offered tantalizing descriptions of exotic places we trade association types would travel to when we worked the annual conventions: Hawaii, Acapulco, and San Francisco. Wow! I also knew that I would be following my heart's desire of writing, as I would be asked to write articles for the association's monthly newsletter. Life was about to get real good. *Wait until the college alumni association hears about me!*

On my first day of work as Ms. Director, I was dressed to direct. I spent what little savings I had from earlier part-time work on some executive accessories. I had the briefcase, the frumpy blue power suit, and the new shoes with the small, sensible heel. I was so pumped! Anxiously, I showed up for work and met all of my new coworkers. Most were recent college graduates like myself. I quickly noticed, however, that I stood alone when it came to peppiness. My colleagues had a bit of frost about them. It was not a happy place. I soon learned why.

While we did go to Acapulco and all those really neat places, and I did practice my writing craft, much of the workday was spent in the bowels of the basement taking part in mind-numbing mass mailings. Our office building was a small, three-story townhouse with a cramped basement that had been converted into a box-laden, paper-strewn mailroom. There were brighter than bright, naked fluorescent bulbs overhead. The smell was dank and musty. It was here that we spent untold hours of our professional existence licking stamps, collating advertising pieces, and stuffing envelopes. Nasty paper cuts and bleeding all over the salutations was par for the course. It was the most boring, low-down, monotonous work I'd ever done in my life. Some days we'd spend all eight hours in this veritable dungeon. We felt a bit like animals in a cage. But we were all at the same point in our careers—the bottom of the ladder. We had to start somewhere. We could have walked out on our Directorships, but that wouldn't have looked good, so most of us hung in there for at least a year.

We were all young go-getters, and the work could not have been more dull. During the mass mailings, we were all on edge by mid-morning. We'd huddle in that glaringly bright, musty, old basement, stuffing envelopes and shooting the breeze. Invariably, the conversation would become a little murky. Gossip was the name of the game. Cruel and crass jokes flew freely. Loud music raged from a portable boom box. Off-color conversations were common. The place was toxic. Really, really toxic.

And this is what *boredom* does to people. An unchallenged, idle mind looks to fill itself with things that excite and titillate. If life seems stale, why not spice it up with some juicy gossip or get a pile of women's magazines and become immersed in the fast, edgy world of celebrities and Hollywood? Better yet, how about some of those steamy, internet websites?

Pornography isn't just a male thing. We don't hear much about women smut consumers. They don't go to strip clubs, nor do they stand around reading magazines in crowded sections of seedy bookstores. But women are buying things through the mail, and they're getting their kicks on-line. As with men in this dangerous pursuit, a little titillation leads to increasingly harsher, more dangerous forms of excitement. Becoming desensitized to one level of stimulation easily flows into the next seedy realm. Every woman who values her sexuality and desires a fulfilling physical relationship in marriage should think very carefully before introducing any form of pornography into the union.

Most of us understand the principle of becoming desensitized—whether it's pornography or violence. My first exposure to violence in films was when I was in second grade and I watched the Oscar award–winning musical, *Oliver!* It's a lovely movie, but there's a scene near the end where a woman named Nancy is beaten to death by a nefarious character played by the late actor, Oliver Reed. What is seen on the screen is the raising and lowering of a cane. What is heard are the anguished cries of the victim. The viewer never sees the cane actually strike the victim, but the implication is clear. That particular scene stuck in my head for years and was quite horrifying to me!

Flash forward to the movie *Carrie,* which I saw in high school in the 1970s. The memorable scene in that movie was when a bucket of animal blood was dumped on a young woman's head at the senior prom. It was a creepy act that sparked an even creepier supernatural rampage. That was scary at the time. Really scary!

Flash forward to recent, popular movies like *Boogie Nights, Kiss the Girls,* and *Seven,* and of course, dozens of other explicit movies—movies filled with hideously graphic sex and violence. These movies make films like *Carrie,* and certainly *Oliver!,* seem like Saturday morning cartoons! Our exposure to gratuitous violence and sex has ratcheted up our shock value. Shock no longer comes easily for today's society, whether it's violence or pornography.

The Bible provides a clear warning about filling our heads with nasty stuff: "Put to death, therefore, whatever belongs to your earthly nature: sexual immorality, impurity, lust, evil desires and greed, which is idolatry. Because of these, the wrath of God is coming" (Colossians 3:5–6).

The traps associated with boredom are more than sensual, pornographic addictions. These are the subtle hazards. Sometimes boredom can turn us into "news hounds" seeking personal information about others that can be used to spice up or enliven conversations. This boredom trap is better known as gossip. And, yes, it's happening at church right now.

Ed Young, senior pastor of Fellowship Church, delivered a sermon touching on the subject of gossip. In the message, he talked about the perils of loose talk and how it can invade the most unlikely places, including Bible study groups. Here's how it goes:

> OK, everyone! We need to bow our heads in prayer. Let's pray first for Mary who's having a real time of it! You see, blah, blah, blah . . .

By prayer's end, everyone knows more about Mary than they needed to know. An innocent prayer, it seems, can even lead to a "little sin."

The Bible speaks on many occasions about idle talk and spreading rumors:

> He who guards his mouth and his tongue keeps himself from calamity (Proverbs 21:23).

> Avoid godless chatter, because those who indulge in it will become more and more ungodly (2 Timothy 2:16).

Even though Todd and I have a great relationship, it has not always been perfect. The first year of marriage was quite challenging as we tried to establish our own identity as a couple and as we tried to figure out how everyone around us fit in. This strain grew increasingly difficult for us over several years of marriage. We did a soft-shoe shuffle around this problem for five years. The issue simply could not be ignored. During this time Todd and I were in an avoidance mode. I, however, had been confiding in friends and family members; and they took sides on the matter. This gossip fanned the flames and brewed up a lot of resentment and anger that could have been avoided had we sought cool-headed, neutral, outside Christian support from the start.

After five years of marriage and an undercurrent in the relationship, I picked up the phone and put in an emotional call to the counselors at Focus on the Family. The staff counselors immediately sized up the situation. They offered to talk to Todd and give him their outside view of the matter. Eventually, they put us in touch with a Christian therapist who helped us develop a course of action that could heal us.

Normally, we don't consider the discussions we have with our friends about our spouses as gossip. But if the husband's not there and we're talking about him, and the nature of the conversation is not positive . . . it is gossip. And, to be sure, it's one of the "little sins."

Some One-on-One Advice

If you have a problem with someone, confront that person in a direct, loving, honest way. Don't whisper behind her back. Don't pull in a third party (other than Christian counselors) into the morass. And, by all means, if the situation involves your spouse, seek professional help. Get some good, Christian support through your church staff or trained counselors. There's no shame in this. If you have a headache, you take a Tylenol. If you cut your finger, you apply a Band-Aid. If there's a fracture in your marriage, get it fixed. Christian counseling can save your union and, in fact, strengthen your relationship in all areas. So it's a godly thing.

When you have time on your hands and boredom sets in, don't default to the remote control or the latest celebrity magazine. Shove your popular media aside and get into God's Word. Some people begin their Bible studies in Genesis and work their way straight through the Bible. I began as more of a random seeker. I searched for wisdom that was applicable to my current situation and used God's Word, along with study guides, to dig into areas of the Bible that I felt were relevant at a given moment in time. That's a start. Whether you take a measured, systematic approach or you want to jump around initially, it really doesn't matter. Pray for God's direction in your spiritual studies and He will lead you where you need to go. You will discover that the Bible is the greatest adventure, mystery, romance, how-to, historical, humor, biography, sociology, suspense, poetry, educational, health, money/finance, scholarly, self-help, love story ever written! It's all there!

Reflections on Boredom

- What are the three activities you "default" to when you are bored?
- Are these activities healthy or unhealthy?
- If any are unhealthy, what are other activities you could be doing instead—things that would strengthen your spiritual well-being and improve your relationships with others?

Blinders and Muzzles:
The Sin of Omission

8

*T*HE DALLAS MORNING NEWS ran an article about a man named Clifford Johnson who wandered the streets of Fort Worth, Texas, every night for thirty years.[1] Clifford knew those streets like the back of his hand. He never had far to go when he was ready to turn in for the night, because the streets were his home. Over the course of three decades, he called Houston Street his bedroom, kitchen, and living room. One bitter cold winter Clifford suffered frostbite. He never walked the same again. Rumor had it, Clifford was once a big-time lawyer. Then something happened, and he cracked up. Local merchants would bring him a warm meal every now and then or a cup of coffee. But mostly, people just whispered. A fellow named Kip Wright, owner of a coffee shop in the area, got tired of all the words in the air. One day he approached Clifford on the street with these words reported by newspaper staff writer Michael E. Young:

"So I asked him one day," Kip recounted to Michael, "I said, 'Clifford, everyone says you're an attorney.'"

Clifford's reply, "No, civil engineer. . . ."

So the silence was broken. Kip learned that Clifford was a white-collar professional working for an aircraft firm when his four-year-old daughter, who was living out of state at the time, drowned in a bathtub. The tragedy derailed Clifford. He closed the book on his world and crawled into the streets. And it took three decades for someone to successfully blow the dust off the cracked binding and bring him back.

Kip took an interest in getting Clifford some help. He knew he would meet resistance if he tried to have him committed to a mental institution. So he assumed a temporary guardianship role to get Clifford off the streets and into a protective environment. This action got the ball rolling in an effort to track down anyone related to Clifford who might provide some more permanent advocacy. A local establishment that catered to disabled street people took Clifford in. Soon family members were located and brought in to help anchor the net of support that was first cast by Kip Wright. He had stepped inside the boundaries of a badly interrupted life and was able to give a man without a home some shelter from the city streets.

Was Kip Wright brilliant, brave, or extraordinarily clever as it related to his efforts to aid Clifford Johnson? Not really. He just took a few extra steps. He went beyond handing out a doughnut and took some responsibility for another person's plight. In today's culture, however, this is a heroic act. A huge deal! If we think about it, it is truly something that almost anyone reading this book could have done. But would we have done it?

A mighty trap of sin that ensnares us relates to the things that we fail to do:

- the wrongdoing that we see and fail to correct,
- the people unjustly torn down whom we don't defend,
- the silence we keep when we ought to speak up,
- the mission to do good that we ignore when it whispers to our heart.

These are but some of the sins of omission. The Bible tells us God is not happy when we look the other way.

The parable of the Good Samaritan talks about a man traveling from Jerusalem to Jericho. On the journey, he was mugged. The robbers stripped off his clothes, beat and abandoned him, leaving him for dead. A priest going down the road saw the poor man and he simply passed him by. Another man approached and he, too, passed by. Then a third man, a despised, half-breed Samaritan walked down this same road. He saw the badly beaten man lying in a heap and took pity on him. He bandaged and medicated his wounds, put the man on his own donkey, and took him to an inn. Then he stayed the entire day with the battered traveler, looking after him. The following day he took out two silver coins and gave them to the innkeeper. "Look after him," he said, "and when I return I will reimburse you for any extra expense you may have."

> Which of these three do you think was a neighbor to the
> man who fell into the hands of robbers? (Luke 10:36)

The answer to the question is obvious. It's hard to understand why so many of us live our lives like the two passersby. Without a doubt, every Christian must ponder whether he or she reflects the graciousness of the Samaritan or the apathy of the passersby.

The sins of omission aren't always a life-altering matter like the one involving Clifford, the homeless man. In our daily life, there are subtle "little sins" of omission—such as overlooking those who need our help.

Our first Fourth of July in Texas was almost more memorable than we bargained for. We're big on celebrations, so we decided to get a rip-roaring assortment of fireworks and have an old-fashioned backyard bash. This was a tradition we carried over from our years in Virginia. We were excited to christen the new yard with some booming, blinding tributes to the U.S.A. We'd done a lot of buildup for our little boys and they were ready for a sky-lighting shower of fun.

The Sunday before the Fourth, I checked the newspaper for fireworks stands and found one several miles away. So we hit the road. My husband picked out a nice assortment of things that made loud noises and other things that flared. I had carefully checked the local newspaper to make sure our plans were legal! There were plenty of articles about the holiday, no mention of illegality, and lots of inserts in the Sunday paper about where to get the best fireworks. So we were set!

On the big night, we pulled our lawn chairs outside, uncoiled the garden hose (just in case), and got an early start on the festivities. The sun wasn't even down, but we were letting the pyrotechnics pop! It was a lovely, warm summer night. Lots of neighbors were out for their evening walk. The community sidewalk is just a few feet from our driveway, so we were within nice talking distance of everyone who passed. We waved to them and even had a chance to chat with some folks we'd never met.

It was a wonderful feeling. Having fun with the family. Meeting the neighbors. One family with a little boy walked by three times. The first time they passed, we introduced ourselves and told them we had recently moved to Texas from Virginia. We learned they were natives who'd just moved from a neighboring town. It was a nice conversation. I noticed the second and third time they passed us that they were really checking out our fireworks. I imagined that they were going to one of the city festivals to watch someone else light the fuses. I felt sorry for the child. I got the sense he would have rather been doing his own thing in the backyard just like us.

By about 9:00 P.M., we were out of ammunition. We picked up what debris we could find, curled up the garden hose, collapsed the lawn chairs, and started to head indoors. Just then I noticed a police car drive slowly by our house. The car stopped briefly. I waved vigorously. Poor police officer! I'll bet he wishes he could be with his family lighting fireworks right now. The cruiser slowly pulled away, and we went inside and got ready for bed. It had been a wonderful celebration.

The next morning I picked up the newspaper. There on the front page was a story about all of the people who'd been nabbed the night before for setting off fireworks illegally. To my dismay and embarrassment, our innocent little celebration had been flat-out illegal. We had broken the law. I would have thought that one of our neighbors would have said something to us, but nothing.

I got this really sick feeling in my stomach as I envisioned what might have happened had we actually been lighting some fuses when the police officer drove past. What if he'd gotten out of his cruiser and told us in front of our little boys that we had broken the law. We'd had many conversations with our little guys about the importance of being good citizens. What kind of indelible impression would have been pasted onto the mind of a four-year-old as he witnessed his mommy and daddy getting into big trouble with a stern-faced uniformed officer?

When we see a wrongdoing that we fail to correct, our nonresponse to a mistake may be harming our neighbor. We, the silent ones, step boldly into other areas of sin if our neighbor (friend, husband, or child) courts trouble that we could have helped them avoid.

Escaping the trap of the sin of omission can involve stepping boldly out of our comfort zones. We human beings like our space. When dogs have a litter of puppies, they crawl all over each other. They sleep on top of one another and nuzzle night and day. We people are quite different. We don't like it when other people get too close. We don't like it when strangers approach us. We just go about our business with *blinders* and *muzzles* and hope that we don't have to engage anyone we don't know as we go about our daily lives. This is partly a reflection of the dangerous times in which we live. But it's also a symptom of our desire to stay at an arm's reach from someone who might want or need something that we don't have the time to give.

Getting involved in other people's lives takes a bit of courage on our part. There are times we need to speak up in the name of love. Speaking up sometimes means getting involved in the lives of people to whom we don't technically "belong." The person in need may be a friend, relative, or someone with whom we have little in common. There are people on the outer fringes whose lives would benefit from the smallest amount of our time and attention.

The region of Texas where we live is referred to as the metroplex. The area covers a number of towns and cities in and around Dallas and Fort Worth. One day, I took my children to a recreation center in a neighboring city. While the boys were running about, I began to chat casually with the mother of a young boy. It was a pleasant but uneventful conversation. After about an hour's time, we went our separate ways, neither of us bonding sufficiently to exchange numbers or anything.

A few weeks later, the boys and I were at a playground in another town nearby. It was a beautiful sunny day. There were a couple dozen mothers and caretakers playing with children. I was pushing two of my little boys on the swings when I caught snippets of conversation between a mother and child occurring right behind me. I could tell that there was a power play in full swing.

"Come here right now!" the mother demanded.

"No!" cried the child.

"I said now!"

"No, I don't want to!"

And on and on it went a few more times. This sort of thing happens all the time, so it was barely noteworthy. But what happened next left an indelible imprint.

"OK. That's it!" I heard the mother say.

The next thing I know a woman brushes past me hauling what looked to be a three- or four-year-old boy like a big bag of sand. She gets to a bench and pulls down his pants, exposing the boy's buttocks. Then she slings him over her knee and gives him six swift whacks . . . this in full view of about twenty dumbstruck adults and twice as many curious children. Now the boy is really mad. He throws himself to the ground and lets out a piercing scream. The woman then drags the poor kid by his arm across the playground, into the parking lot, deposits him into a minivan, and drives off.

My jaw was just sort of hanging unhinged on my face as I tried to figure out where in the world I had seen this woman. She looked so familiar. Then it occurred to me—this was the woman I chatted with at the recreation center a few weeks earlier.

I didn't hang around the playground much longer. The public spanking incident sullied the morning for me. I had a hard time shaking the image of this humiliating spectacle.

About a month later, I was at yet another park in a different city. It was now late June and getting hot in Texas so playground traffic was light. We arrived mid-morning and we had the place to ourselves. About fifteen minutes later, a little boy came running in. He zipped over to my boys and began helping himself to my children's toys piled in the stroller. I thought to myself, *I might expect this from a two-year-old, but this child was too old to be grabbing a stranger's things without invitation.* Then, about thirty seconds later, who rounds the corner? You guessed it! The public spanker!

"Oh! I remember you!" she said to me cheerily.

"Really," I mumbled.

"Yes! Didn't we meet about a month ago?"

"You could be right," I replied, avoiding eye contact and quickly concocting in my mind an exit strategy. This was not a woman I wanted to chat up.

"Sure is hot," she said.

By now, I was briskly gathering up our belongings and stuffing them back into the stroller. Her son was pulling things out as quickly as I was putting them away. The mother did nothing to intervene.

"You have three boys, right?" she asked.

"I do," I said, never looking up.

I called to my children, "Do you want some juice?" This was my attempt to get the focus on the kids and off this going-nowhere-fast friendship. I began pulling out some box drinks, when her little boy rushed me and grabbed one of the juice boxes in my hand. The next thing I know, he was diving into my children's snacks. The mother noticed and very gently told the little boy to retreat, but he just ignored her. I'm thinking to myself, *Uh oh! When are the pants coming down? Is she going to do it again?* Instead, for the next couple of minutes, she tried using her words.

"Are you bothered by something?" she said to the little boy who was practically on top of me trying to get at our stuff.

"Are you tired?" she asked very carefully. "Let's get to the root of it."

By now, I'd had enough of the boy and sure didn't want to encourage this mother. I packed everyone up and politely, but determinedly, positioned myself to make a break for it. We were still relatively new to Texas and I could have used a few more friends, but, of all the bad luck, to run into this woman three different times in three different cities in as many months!

We left the park and continued about our day. Unlike the time before, I didn't give our morning encounter too much additional thought. That night, however, I got into bed and began praying. For some reason, my thoughts returned to this mother and son. Then something struck me. *I suddenly wondered if I had missed an opportunity. Instead of giving these people the brush-off, should I have embraced them? Should I have taken some time to get to know her? Could I have made a difference in her life?* I'm not a perfect mother and I certainly don't have all the right answers, but a few encounters with this lady suggested to me that she badly needed some empathy and kindness.

I was now feeling sorry for passing by this woman. I was reminded, again, of the parable of the Good Samaritan. While this woman wasn't lying in a heap beside the road, there was something dispirited about her. I sensed she was lonely and probably would have benefited from having someone to talk to. Maybe I could have helped her. Maybe I could have told her about the easy and fun incentive program we use in our home to keep the boys on track. Maybe I could have told her about the great church we attend. Maybe I could have shared the secret of my own joy and peace, which comes from faith in Christ. Maybe, with the smallest investment of my time, I could have made a difference in her life and the life of her little boy. Yet . . . I passed her by.

I was reminded of the times in my own life as a mother when I was disheartened, lonely, and starved for adult conversation. Suddenly the feeling of superiority that led me to ever so slightly tilt my head and walk away from this woman evaporated like fog in the sun. I could vividly see a big piece of myself in her.

God knows my heart. He knows the immense capacity and will I have to give. I can only imagine His disappointment in the knowledge that I willfully dusted away a perfect opportunity to serve Him when I closed the door on this woman and her child.

I remember another opportunity I had to get involved. I was at the public library with my children one day. We were standing at the front desk about twenty feet from the entrance. I was trying to complete my transaction with the librarian while keeping an eye on my children who were bustling about behind me. At one point, I turned to look at the boys and noticed a small figure coming through the doorway. I took my eyes off my children for a moment and all but audibly gasped at the sight. The small figure entering the library belonged to that of a woman who looked like a walking skeleton draped in skin. I was so stunned by her appearance, I couldn't take my eyes off of her despite the fact we had made eye contact and she knew I was staring at her. Though she was obviously a young woman and probably at one time very beautiful, her skin clung to the bones in her face and carved deep, exaggerated hollows. She walked with the frailty of a ninety-year-old woman. I was sure I was looking at someone who was near death from anorexia.

After a moment, I composed myself and smiled at her to conceal my shock. Then I flashed to my own history with an eating disorder. I searched my brain wildly for something to say or do that might help this poor woman. But nothing was coming to me. My heart was racing. I was poised to say something, but my mind went utterly blank. The librarian handed me my books. I corralled the boys and began to head in the direction of the doors. As I passed this woman, all I could do was force a smile and mutter, "Hello."

Hello?

There was hardly a day that passed that I didn't think about this woman and what I failed to do. It wasn't a conscious failure on my part. I desperately wanted to do something. I just didn't know what to do. I was unprepared.

I pledged after that encounter to be prepared for the next brush with someone in need. Rather than relying upon a brain that might default to a blank slate, I would have my "foot-in-the-door opening" formulated in advance. One can hardly accost a stranger with the words "You look like you are an anorexic. Is there anything I can do for you?" Instead, I would zone in on an external feature—shoes, hairstyle, purse, watch—and use this as an icebreaker to strike a dialogue with that individual. "Do you have the time? What a neat watch! I love those shoes. Where did you get them?" Once the portal of communication was opened, I would rely upon God to help do the rest and pray that He would help me find the next string of words that might allow me to get into this person's world and perhaps help.

After spotting that woman in the library, I prayed from time to time that I might see her again and have a second chance, somehow, to get involved. A couple months after that sad and stunning first encounter, I was back at the library with my children. We were heading to the checkout desk with an armful of books when I spotted that same small figure in one of the aisles reaching for something on a shelf. I stopped nearly dead in my tracks and did a computer-like brain scan trying to come up with my words of entry. Was there something she was wearing or doing that could get me an introduction into her world? It was a hot summer afternoon and the library was as crowded as I've ever seen it. My thoughts quickly went from: *What can I say?* to *How on earth am I going to do this in front of all of these people?* Then my mind went into a kind of sleep mode much like it had done before. So much for being prepared.

Another thought crossed my mind: *What if I'm wrong? What if she has some other health problem and I'm about to embarrass the both of us?* For a moment, I forgave myself this latest mental meltdown and felt a sense of personal relief that perhaps her problem was not what I thought it was. Then a haunting thought returned: *But what if I'm right?* Whatever momentary relief I felt as I mentally processed the possible scenarios was now replaced with a sick, sad feeling in my heart. I was about to blow it again!

I was still standing there kind of stuck in a mental rut when the woman suddenly turned and looked at me and offered a gentle smile. I returned the smile and tried to hold eye contact with her in hopes she would hang in there with me until I could find the right words. I was desperate to say something, but nothing was coming to me. In a moment's time, the woman turned from me and continued to search for something on a shelf. I missed my chance.

I walked with the boys over to the front desk, checked out my books, and proceeded slowly and dejectedly out of the library. With each step, it felt as if a field of gravity was trying to pull me back. My legs did not want to walk my body out of that building. But I couldn't bear the thought of turning around and coming face-to-face with this person and thirty others. So I kept on going.

On the way to the car, my little boys were chattering in unison. It was just background noise for me. I didn't hear a word they said because I was just overflowing with disappointment over this second chance that I'd prayed for and summarily cast to the wind. I helped the boys into their car seats and prayed that God would give me the guts to do something while I still had a chance. Then, I looked on the passenger seat and saw a piece of paper and a red pen. I knew immediately what had to be done. My mouth had failed me, but my pen would not.

I secured the boys in the back of the car, then bolted into the driver's seat and picked up that pen. I had no idea how much time I had, but I knew I needed to work fast. I prayed to God that every word coming off the tip of that pen would be right. I didn't want to offend this woman, but I had to gently suggest to her that she appeared to need help. I told her I'd seen her once before and was struck by how lovely she was, yet so thin. I asked her to forgive my intrusion, but I wrote that I could see myself in her. I told her about my own experience with bulimia and how God had saved my life. And I told her I wanted to help her if, in fact, she was somehow suffering. I left my name and number and encouraged her to call.

As I penned the last several digits of my phone number, I prayed: *God, just let her walk out. Let her walk out. Let her walk out,* because I wasn't sure I had the grit to go back in that building and confront her amidst a crowd. I no sooner mentally uttered those words to God in prayer than I looked up and there she was about to cross the street into the parking lot. I flung open my car door and strode briskly toward her, folding my note as I walked. She was on the curb about to step into the street and I called out gently, "Excuse me . . ." She stopped and gave a small tentative smile.

"This is for you," I said as I handed her the note. "I saw you once before, and I wish I'd given this to you then." The smile briefly left her face. I had a sense she somehow knew what she was about to read. I patted her gently on the arm before I turned to go back to my car. I had to force myself to smile to keep from cringing at the feeling I experienced when my hand touched her arm. It was literally skin and bone.

"Thank you," she softly called to me.

As I got into my car, I began to cry. I didn't want her to see my tears, so I looked down and tried to appear like I was reading something. I looked over once briefly and could see that she was now in her car some distance away in the parking lot. I imagined she was reading my note, but I couldn't tell for sure. I waited a couple of minutes in hopes that she might get a head start on me so she wouldn't see the sadness staining my face. But she wasn't leaving. So I put the car in drive and slowly began to move out of the parking lot. As I approached the exit, I turned to look at her. She put a small, fragile hand up to the glass of her window as I drove past and held it there briefly. I raised my hand to her and smiled through trembling lips. I wanted to stop my car and just run over to this woman and hug her, but I knew I couldn't force this connection. She could all too easily just slip away. The next move would have to happen on her terms and in her own time and space.

Sadly, I am still waiting for the phone to ring.

How I wish I had a storybook ending to share with you. How I wish I could say that she called, we met, and we talked. I wish I could tell you that I took her to my church. I wish I could tell you that I sat across from her at lunch—possibly, the first real lunch in two years. But I don't have that ending to the story.

Not yet anyway.

My actions were small and potentially of little or no consequence. But I refuse to cross this encounter off as a failed or fruitless effort, because the outcome of this story remains open. I believe that God does indeed work in mysterious ways. I have hope in my heart that something good can still come from two stunning and poignant encounters with a stranger. I pray almost daily that I will see that woman again. And I feel that, indeed, I will. The next time, my actions are bound to be more confident and steady. Because we connected, I can approach her now with purpose and familiarity. I pray that God will reward my faithfulness and patience with another chance. Maybe she will call. Maybe I'll see her again at the library. Maybe God will eventually work through me to help lift her up and out of the earthly hell I suspect she inhabits.

So I wait in hopes that God is still working this one out. I also close my eyes at night and feel none of the guilt or frustration I felt after that first encounter. I feel instead a sense of satisfaction and peace about what I tried to do for better or worse. I am hopeful, if not optimistic, that there will be a next time when God determines that the time is right.

I carry in my purse a small note in an envelope addressed to: *a friend.* It's a note I may give to this woman when and if I see her again. In it I tell her that I still want to hear from her if she ever feels like talking. The letter also has my address and e-mail so that she has a safe way to reach me if talking on the phone or face-to-face is too threatening or uncomfortable for her. I hope I never have to give her this letter. I pray that the next time I see her all the right words will just roll off my lips. But in case they don't . . . I'm ready.

Reflections on Omissions

- Have you ever failed to speak up when you saw someone doing something wrong?
- Why did you keep silent?
- Would you respond to that situation differently today?

Nothing Left to Give: The Sin of Indolence

9

WE LIVE IN a fast-paced world. As we chase after greater levels of prosperity and power there's not much "left over" for the Lord's work. Most of us barely have enough time for our immediate family, let alone other relatives and friends. If we were to create a "make-time-for" to-do list, at the very bottom would probably be: *make time for those in need.* Our thoughts about this list, if they could be revealed, would probably be something like this: *"I'd love to do it! But my plate is full. I just don't have the time. Some day . . ."*

In the previous chapter, we looked at the sin of omission. The action we consciously fail to take when we should have done something. While the sin of indolence appears to be similar, it differs from the sin of omission in the way it relates to our commitments. Sins of omission usually don't involve much of our time. It's refusing to disclose to the uninformed neighbor that backyard fireworks are illegal. It's not telling someone his or her front tire looks low on air. It's not helping someone avoid a trap that we clearly see and they don't. The sin of omission is more often a missed opportunity to jump in and do something corrective.

However, the sin of indolence is rooted in more of a commitment and continuum. It is letting the fast-paced, stressful, material-oriented world rob us of the energies needed to serve those who can't return the favor. The dictionary defines *indolence* as a "disinclination to exert oneself." A synonym is laziness. I know some are asking how can I speak of laziness when we're working harder, sleeping less, and finding no quality time for our family or ourselves. How can we be lazy in this fast-paced, roller-coaster, stressed-out, frazzled world?

The truth is, we have a selective energy. We can find the time to work longer hours and enjoy prolonged entertainment, but when it comes to finding time to help someone who's less fortunate we, somehow, just can't find the time. This is the sin of indolence. To live a truly God-inspired life, however, we have to make room in our lives to serve. There's not a cookie-cutter formula that tells us who and how to serve. It's up to each of us to assess our skills and talents and come up with the right outlet. Then . . . we must make time, which probably means we must give something up.

When my third child, Daniel, was a baby, I breast-fed him in front of cable television in the middle of the night. Caring for two toddlers and a baby during the day left little time for normal television viewing beyond *Barney*. So, I actually enjoyed getting up in the wee hours and channel surfing. I would catch headline news or sound bytes from talk shows and movies. This somehow took me outside of my at-home bubble and plugged me into the world.

I remember one night I landed on a rerun of a popular talk show. I stayed with the program long enough to let it rattle me to the core. The talk show's guests were women—wives and mothers—who had decided to put the focus of life back on themselves and place the needs of others on the back burner. While these guests talked a happy story about fulfillment in the land of "me," their faces told a different story. There was not an ounce of true joy about them. They had taken charge of their lives and no one was going to stand in the way of satisfying their own needs. At times, it seemed that they were struggling to believe their own rhetoric.

Beyond what the panel was espousing, I was even more surprised and saddened by the reaction this message was drawing. The talk show host and the audience were just feeding upon it. Cameras throughout the program were cutting away to focus on the slack-jawed, bug-eyed audience participants soaking up the advice. The host chimed in with an occasional "Wow!" The electricity around this program could have lit up a stadium. People were visibly digesting every wayward morsel. And let's face it . . . we all crave joy in our lives, don't we? This show jabbed and poked at this nerve with a magical "me" plan for good living. I have no doubt that more than a few audience members and television viewers set off on a course to find an inner joy that could only stretch and deepen the void in their soul.

When I brood on what the road holds for those who are grasping at straws of joy in "me-focus" I am deeply saddened. We have to look no further than God's Word to find that this is the road to nowhere. The Bible tells us that contentment and true peace are not derived from earthly sources of focus or pleasure, but from God alone: "Peace, I leave with you; my peace I give you. I do not give to you as the world gives" (John 14:27).

Thankfully, God gives us His peace. And He, at the same time, calls on us to *give* to others. "It is more blessed to give then to receive" (Acts 20:35). God is a God of giving and He wants us to be a giving people.

I'm often reminded of the days when I thought only of

myself—the single years when all I had was a career to think about. I remember my beauty routine in those days. I spent thirty minutes putting on makeup in the morning, using every shadow-and-light trick I'd learned from the half-a-dozen women's magazines I used to read. After my eyelashes were sufficiently separated and curled and the rest of my face was shimmering in pink and purple goop, I moved on to my hair. This took another thirty minutes depending upon how many times I would need to re-curl, re-brush, re-fluff or respray. The focus was *me*.

I also remember gift shopping when I slowly cruised the aisles for two hours or more to find the perfect gift. I remember quiet time in those days when I would spend hours and hours watching talk shows and chick flicks in the solitude of my peaceful, motionless living room. I didn't have to share a remote with a man and there were no wailing babies flailing about. All I had back then was time and space to myself. And do you know what? I was miserable! I had life all to myself and it made for a very sad, superficial, and bleak existence.

Today, it's a good day if I get out of the house with a slathering of sunscreen and a swipe of frosty mocha lipstick that's actually staining my lips as opposed to my teeth. My hair has a mind of its own which is both independent and insane. I purchase most gifts in a mad, impulsive, beast-like sprint through the store. And I haven't watched a daytime talk show in years. But I've never been happier, because the balance in my life is hanging in the direction of God's will, not my own. While I still have those days that challenge the soul, I have a direction and a purpose in life that gets me through the bad patches and a perspective of gratitude and joy that shines over the rest of my days.

When I get into trouble it's often because I'm chasing the elusive state of: *"Me . . . and I can have it all."* When the *taking* outnumbers the *giving,* I find myself swimming up to my bleary eyeballs in guilt. As I try to achieve Christ-centered wellness in my life, I regularly take a personal inventory of what really matters to me. I rank what matters in importance from most to least. Then I indulge happily and guilt-free in what I can realistically enjoy without compromising the major priorities of life: God, marriage, and family. In doing so, I also have to be willing to just let some things go. Because the *"Me . . . and I can have it all"* syndrome is just a ghost when it comes to earthly derived sources of happiness. There's no such thing.

One important aspect of living as Christ intended is making the time to get out of my nest and serve the needs of others beyond my own immediate family. I mentioned earlier that when God restored me to health after many years of struggling with bulimia that I strongly sensed that He was not done with me. I knew at the time that God would expect something in return. In time, I would grow to realize that God wanted me to change the focus of my life from *taking* to *giving,* and this would mean that I was to seek out and find avenues to help others as He had helped me.

This "giving" tug started out as a whisper in my heart. Over time, it became more of a shout. At some point, I knew that I would never return to the corporate world. I was done lusting after promotions and pay raises. My life's work would be waged on a different front. I would do my best to serve the Lord wherever and whenever I could. This book is one such example. I never thought I would disclose for public consumption the raw and tortured saga of a thirteen-year battle with bulimia. I never thought I would write a book about sin. But this is the direction that God has led me. It's a way I can help others and, by extension, serve the Lord.

Throughout the Bible, much is made of God's expectation that we lend a hand to those in need. This is more than tithing. This is rolling up our sleeves and taking *action,* even if it's only an hour a week. We have to make the time for others. It may mean cutting back on something—work time or play time—to free up our schedules for time to serve others. I've discovered an awesome, life-changing benefit in doing the Lord's work. When I focus my attention on the people around me who are needy, I dwell less on the superficial things in my own life that might bring me down. Volunteering makes me feel good . . . and there are no unpleasant side effects!

In the book of James, God's Word makes this point: "You see that a person is justified by what he does and not by faith alone" (James 2:24). This verse is about taking action. Walking the talk! Putting our money where our mouth is! Getting the wheels in motion!

A former high-flying Dallas computer executive named Doug Freeman took an early retirement several years ago to concentrate on his spiritual development.[2] He took up religious studies and earned a degree from a local seminary. Then he embarked upon a heavenly paved path to uplift and encourage the elderly. Doug, who is now a pastor, developed the program—"Be-A-Pal"— which pairs church volunteers with lonely seniors. Once a week Doug helps a group of senior citizens board a bus bound for the local mall where they can browse and shop. He tells the story of the time he helped a group of geriatric women with failing eyesight work their way through the lingerie department. They were unable to discern an A cup from a D cup, so Doug helped them secure some nicely fitted bras and panties. All in a day's work! Though he had climbed on top of the corporate ladder and walked away with bags of money, he says working with the elderly is by far the most rewarding job of his life.

Doug Freeman is a volunteer who is twice blessed. He's getting plenty of notice, I presume, from God for his good works! And he's receiving lots of grateful feedback from the people he serves.

There are times, though, when attempts to serve may not be recognized or appreciated. Not everyone responds to gifts with glee. I've known people who have gone to considerable lengths to serve others and found that their kindness was barely acknowledged. This can be hurtful and, at worst case, cause the giver to regret giving. But we must remember that warm and fuzzy "thank-you's" are not the point. While everyone wants to feel appreciated, God wants our volunteer spirit to be based upon a different fundamental:

> Be careful not to do your acts of righteousness before men, to be seen by them. If you do, you will have no reward from your Father in heaven. So when you give to the needy, do not announce it with trumpets, as the hypocrites do in the synagogues and on the streets, to be honored by men. I tell you the truth, they have received their reward in full. But when you give to the needy, do not let your left hand know what your right hand is doing, so that your giving may be in secret. Then your Father, who sees what is done in secret, will reward you (Matthew 6:1–4).

God wants us to be humble givers. He tells us that if our motivation to give is all about getting patted on the back and exalted on earth, we have missed the boat. We will not be credited for these things in heaven. But the things we do in secret will be praised and rewarded by God.

The stories coming out of the Honduran flood of the late 1990s made me sick. When I heard about a young girl sent by her parents to retrieve food from a central relief station, my heart broke into a billion pieces. The little girl, who had no shoes, walked for hours to get to the place. By the time she arrived, food was scarce. The workers gave her one egg and a small bottle of cooking oil—this for a family of seven.

I decided to mobilize my neighbors, friends, and family around a small grassroots relief effort. I got on the phone and tried to track down someone who might be spearheading a relief effort locally. I contacted television and radio stations, and various local government agencies before I landed on a small Hispanic church that was planning to run a busload of emergency supplies to Honduras in three days. I printed up a flyer and popped it in the neighbors' mailboxes. I got on the phone to friends and family. Then I offered up my house as a collection point . . . and people responded.

I probably put about two hours of time into the whole effort. I certainly didn't break a sweat. It was such a small thing to do. But you should have seen the boxes and bags of things sitting in our living room. The room was filled with love. And we didn't need a committee to tell us how to do it. We didn't need someone's permission. We didn't have to wait for detailed instructions on how to proceed. We just *did* it. And so can you!

The sin of indolence has a tendency to spill into our purses and wallets. My husband came home from work one night and told me over dinner about a man he heard on talk radio. He was a highly paid physician who cheerfully talked about giving away most of his earnings to those who had desperate needs. He more than adequately provided for his family—they had a house, clothes, and food. But there was nothing to speak of in the bank, though he admitted he earned a hefty salary as a busy doctor. The man said he gave tens of thousands of dollars away each year. He said he wasn't concerned about running out of money because he knew that when the need presented itself, God would help him find a way.

While this is an extreme example of giving, it did make me think about my own charitable commitments.

Some One-on-One Advice

Can you give up a few accessories—bangles, baubles, new clothes, costly cosmetics—if it means you have a little extra to give? Can you put a moratorium on pizza delivery for a couple of weeks and donate the money to a food pantry? Can you raid your closet and give the local women's shelter some clothes you haven't worn in years? Can you, monthly, dedicate $25.00 of food for the poor from your grocery-shopping trip?

Examine your finances. Get your arms around what you have. Then pray for the courage to let some things go. If giving is not in your nature, don't feel as if you have to go out tomorrow, sell your grandmother's china, hock your diamond ring, and give up a spare kidney. Start small if you need to. But start somewhere! Begin giving. Commit to giving regularly. Make it a monthly habit, just as you may have made savings a habit. Then, over time, your comfort level with giving will increase and you will move closer to the *cheerful* giving state that Jesus wills for us as recorded in Second Corinthians.

> Remember this: Whoever sows sparingly will also reap sparingly, and whoever sows generously will also reap generously. Each man should give what he has decided in his heart to give, not reluctantly or under compulsion, for God loves a cheerful giver (2 Corinthians 9:6–7).

Reflections on Indolence

- Have you ever ignored a tug at your heart to help someone in need? If so, why?
- Is there someone in your life today who needs you?
- Will you help her or him? Why or why not?
- If you are willing to help, what specifically will you do?

What Are We Really Saying?: The Sin of Broken Promises and Empty Words

10

MY FRIEND LORI loves to give to others and she's good at it. One October, she made a wonderful dinner for us and outfitted our boys in some costumes that her own children had outgrown. As I received these items from Lori, I told her that I would get her casserole dishes back to her quickly and return the costumes, too. A couple weeks went by and I called Lori on the phone.

"Lori," I said, "I'm sorry about not getting your things back to you. I'll do it this week."

"That's great. Please keep the costumes, though," she said.

Still I had those casserole dishes to deal with. Well, the week came and went. The next week passed. Before long, two months had gone by, and every time I hit the brakes for a stoplight I could hear the clank of Lori's casserole lid as it slid into the side of my trunk. I would grimace and hope it was still in one piece as I tenderly hit the accelerator when the light turned green. I was swimming in guilt over the fact I had failed to keep my word.

I've found it's all too easy to break the little commitments. This isn't about staying true to marriage vows or making mortgage payments, but the garden-variety promises that may or may not be kept.

We have a euphemistic expression about keeping our word—we call it "follow through." When someone fails to live up to a little commitment, we often say, "She simply didn't follow through." Sounds pretty harmless, doesn't it? So-and-so didn't break a promise nor did she lie—she just failed to follow through. But what does all this mean when we take off the protective coating?

If I've said I'm going to do something, I've made a promise which is the assurance that I will or will not do something. If I don't honor that assurance, I've broken the promise. A broken promise is fundamentally a lie. And a lie is a sin.

What does failure to "follow through" look like? I kept watch over a variety of promises broken in my own life and this is what I recorded:

- One baby-sitter was a no-show.
- One baby-sitter left with a "credit due" and she never came back.
- One cleaning lady quit with no notice.
- The friend who referred the cleaning lady promised to get to the bottom of situation and never did.
- One cleaning lady missed an appointment then called eight hours later.
- Several "let me call you right back" promises never happened.
- Two contractors were no-shows.

The broken promises listed above were a result of carelessness about keeping promises. Contemporary society has reached a point where promises don't mean much anymore. Many of us freely break the commitments we make . . . and no one is holding us accountable.

I took the list I just noted and recounted the many times that I've fallen into the same trap. I've promised to do something or be somewhere and failed to live up to my own words. I also analyzed my response to each of these situations and found that I am partially to blame for "enabling" these situations to occur again and again.

- One baby-sitter was a no-show.
  My response: Crossed her off my baby-sitting list.

- One baby-sitter left with a "credit due" and she never came back.
  My response: Called the mother a couple months later to find out what happened.

- One cleaning lady quit with no notice.
  My response: Put in a couple of calls that were not returned and asked a friend to find out what happened.

- The friend who referred the cleaning lady promised to get to the bottom of situation and never did.
  My response: Nothing.

- One cleaning lady missed an appointment and called eight hours late. *My response: Crossed her off my cleaning lady list.*

- Several "let me call you right back" promises never happened.
  My response: Nothing.

- Two contractors were no-shows.
  My response: Found a different contractor.

As one can tell, I have a pattern of letting people off the hook with the greatest of ease. There is virtually no accountability imposed on my behalf for any of these people who fail to keep their word. I came to the startling conclusion that I am letting people walk all over me. What's worse, within my own little orbit, I am perpetuating a destructive "make it or break it" cycle by not doing a better job of holding people accountable for the pledges they make. People let me down. Sometimes it's annoying, but when it involves friends or loved ones, it can be disappointing and even painful. But what am I doing about it? Not much!

If I had taken each of the noted situations and, kindly but firmly, let these people know they failed to "make good" on their word, it might make them think about future commitments. I'm not naïve enough to suggest that we have the power to alter the behavior of someone who has no regard for keeping the truth. But somehow we must convince others and ourselves that a broken commitment is the same as a broken promise and that is sin.

There's another issue that grows out of good intentions and empty words. "Let me know if there's anything I can do for you," we say. These are words I've expressed many times myself. In retrospect, I could count on one hand the number of times people have actually taken me up on my offer. They probably see my offer as polite, but passive.

When people are in trouble, they usually don't know what they need. I learned through a very painful event that it's sometimes better to approach someone in crisis with tangibles.

The phone rang late one night. I was drifting into sleep and faintly remember Todd getting out of bed to answer the call. The next thing I remember is seeing Todd's silhouette in the dark. He was sitting on the edge of the bed and I could see that his head was in his hands. I knew the news was not good.

"What is it?" I asked softly.

"My dad just called," Todd answered. His voice was tender and full of emotion. "There was a car accident and my mom didn't make it."

Todd's parents were driving to the post office to mail Christmas packages that afternoon when their car was hit broadside by a police cruiser a block from their suburban Chicago home. Todd's dad was taken to intensive care and his mom, a vibrant woman with energy and passion for living, died in the emergency room four hours later.

The shocking and sudden nature of this tragedy threw our family into a state of crisis. Todd flew to Chicago to be with his father the next morning. The boys and I stayed in Texas and tried to comfort Todd over the phone. But long distance love just wasn't cutting it. We needed to be with him. I shoved some clothes in duffel bags, piled the boys into the car, and we set out on a one-thousand-mile journey.

Friends from church questioned the sanity and safety of this long drive. There were many tangible offers of aid:

"Let me drive with you."

"Let me fly with you."

"Let me watch the boys while you pack."

"Let us keep the boys for you."

"I'm bringing over some dinner."

"Let me pray with you right now."

"I want to go to the store for you. What do you need?"

"I've got the tire shop holding four tires. Let's get you over there so they can look at your car."

If my friends had said to me, "Let me know if there's anything I can do for you," I would have said, "It's under control, thank you."

But the fact is it wasn't under control. Todd's grief was such that he wasn't thinking clearly. I was setting out on a two-day journey with three small children and bad tires. I needed help badly. I just didn't know what it was that I needed. But my blessed friends mobilized and did the thinking for me.

Now when I come face-to-face with people who are suffering, I am more careful with my words. Sometimes I am tempted to say, "Let me know if there is anything I can do for you," because that's what I've always said. Now, I look for ways to help. If the answer is not obvious to me, I recast that question by asking, "What can I do to help?" Then I work this question until I come up with something concrete. Sometimes the support needed is a shared prayer. Other times it's a home-made pasta dinner or a devotional book to read.

I was forever touched and changed by the kindness of friends in my own life. I learned that there's a big difference between words and actions. We can all talk. More importantly, we can also act.

Forgotten commitments, broken promises, empty words, and failure to follow-up—we've all been there. These may not seem like big issues. But they have a way of chipping away at our integrity. They also weaken our defenses to spiritual attack.

There's an old nursery rhyme from the 17th century that makes the point in a lovely and simple way:

A man of words and not of deeds
Is like a garden full of weeds.
And when the weeds begin to grow,
It's like a garden full of snow.[3]

So pull some weeds and let God's sunshine melt the snow!

Reflections on Broken Promises and Empty Words

- Can you recall the last time you broke a promise or failed to keep a commitment? What kept you from being true to your word?
- Do you remember a time you had to lovingly confront someone? How did you feel afterward?
- Do you remember a time you failed to confront someone in need of correction? How did you feel afterward?
- Is there action in your life as it relates to helping others, or do you rely primarily on your words?

SIN Less

11

B Y NOW, WE'VE SEEN enough Scriptural evidence to know that God doesn't have a sliding scale for our sins. There's no big sin. No medium sin. No little sin. Sin is sin. So whether we are breaking our marriage vows or failing to follow through on a promise to return a neighbor's garden hoe, we have sinned in the eyes of God.

Maybe you're wondering, as I did: how will I *ever* get to a level of discernment required to stop plowing into the many silent traps? What can I do? Sin is all around me like a toxic, invisible cloud. How can I live a life pleasing to God—with purity and morality?

Beginning in this chapter, I propose a battle plan for relaxing the grip of sin on our daily lives. It's a plan that begins with a simple and blunt acronym that you will read about shortly, but first let me offer this biblical encouragement.

> For the LORD gives wisdom, and from his mouth come knowledge and understanding. . . . Then you will understand what is right and just and fair—every good path. For wisdom will enter your heart, and knowledge will be pleasant to your soul. Discretion will protect you, and understanding will guard you (Proverbs 2:6, 9–11).

Spiritual wisdom will open your eyes and give you discernment for sidestepping the traps of sin. If you're a Christian and struggling with sin in your life, you need to pray to the Lord, asking Him to increase your wisdom and knowledge about sin. He will, through the Holy Spirit, give you discretion about the traps of sin waiting to ensnare you. This understanding will guard you as you acquire the ability to avoid these traps.

God has given you free will. He won't keep you from making bad choices about your own response to certain situations. Remember David and Bathsheba? As with David, God will reveal both life's big and little sins to you. And if you do make the wrong choice and fall prey to sin, the Holy Spirit will let you know, in no uncertain terms, that you have sinned.

When God made me aware of the little sins in my life, I decided to write this book to warn others. My eyes were open wide to sin's traps. But, one day a neighbor stopped by the house and we began chatting. The conversation slipped into a bit of gossip. I said some things about another individual that shouldn't have been said. As the words were coming out of my mouth, I wanted to stuff them back in. Of course, it was too late. I said what I said, and I knew I had sinned. In the past, I could have easily rationalized this encounter as something my neighbor needed to know about a mutual acquaintance. Or, I could have dismissed the whole conversation as a bunch of harmless girl talk. But it wasn't harmless, and she didn't need to know. I sinned. And the Holy Spirit let me know in no uncertain terms that I had messed up.

To reach this level of sensitivity in my own life, prayer was a crucial first step. I pray for God's forgiveness for all aspects of sin . . . that which is obvious and that which is hidden from me. Then I appeal to Him to help me better understand the areas of my life where I may be weak and blind to the traps.

There are other tactics that can help us. I propose a battle plan for getting around sin in our daily lives. It springs forth from a simple acronym: SIN Less. My prayer is that everyone reading this book will develop a greater discernment for the little sins in our midst; and that they will become glaringly obvious. For now, remember the acronym!

S . . . Scrutinize
I . . . Inspire
N . . . Neutralize

S Is for Scrutinize

12

I HAD MY OWN wake-up call regarding scrutiny and truth not too long ago. It was a Saturday morning and Todd and the boys were at Home Depot doing whatever it is that men do at Home Depot on Saturday mornings. I was working on a cup of coffee and cleaning the kitchen. I had Christian radio turned on and someone was singing a song about Christ being "worthy" of our praise. A couple days earlier, I'd seen a magazine article that used the word "worthy" to describe God. The week before, one of our pastors led a prayer exalting Jesus as "worthy."

Each time I heard the word *worthy* used in the same breath as God, it struck me as peculiar. But hearing three references in the space of a week began to bother me. I imagined a rookie athlete coming face-to-face with his sports hero and uttering the words, "Dude! You are worthy!" I imagined a daughter looking into her father's eyes and saying, "I love you, Dad. You are worthy!" To my thinking, it just didn't work.

I had spent the better part of twenty years working with written language, so words really meant something to me. All this "worthy" talk was starting to make me very uncomfortable. I was sure I'd uncovered some sort of new age plot to diminish God by demoting him from Almighty to something in the mid-range of an employee performance review.

I made a beeline to my computer and dashed off an emotional letter to Hank Hanegraaff, the Bible Answer Man. In the note, I decried the use of the word "worthy" in relation to God and appealed to him to get that word off the airways and out of the pulpits. I wrapped it up quickly and was surfing for an e-mail address so I could zap it along just as Todd walked in the door. I rushed over to him with a copy of my letter. I could feel that I was red in the face and breathing hard over the indignity of it all. I explained to Todd that it was nothing short of blasphemy. Todd, who still had some Home Depot glow about him, let me go on for a couple of minutes without interruption. Then he calmly said to me:

"That's very interesting. What does the Bible say about it?"

I could feel my face just kind of fall. "I don't really know," I replied. With that, I slowly approached the book table where I kept my Bible and flipped to the concordance. I could feel my eyes involuntarily squint the way they do when I'm about to view something I really don't want to see. There I noted the use of the word *worthy* as it was used to describe God in Hebrews, First Corinthians, Revelation, and other books of the Bible. Come to find out, it's a word that God used to describe Himself.

I never did find an e-mail address for Hank Hanegraaff the morning I wrote that note about my impressions of God's worthiness. Fortunately, I was spared the embarrassment of sending a foolish letter to the Bible Answer Man. I share this story not because I delight in egg on my face, but because I wanted to illustrate through my own mistakes that we walk on shaky ground when we allow feelings and perceptions to drive our thoughts and actions. Scrutiny is an essential requirement to earthly and spiritual understanding and wisdom.

The dictionary defines *scrutinize* as: "to examine closely, to search, to carefully look over, and analyze."

An appropriate Bible verse is: "Dear friends, do not believe every spirit, but test the spirits to see whether they are from God" (1 John 4:1, see also Acts 17:11).

I talked about validating our impulses in chapter 6 and taking the big *time-out*. That's an earthly tactic we should constantly employ in our lives. But there's a divine aid that's infinitely more powerful in the drive to scrutinize our motives—the gift of wisdom. Proverbs tells us:

> Call out for insight and cry aloud for understanding, and if you look for it as for silver and search for it as for hidden treasure, then you will understand the fear of the Lord and find the knowledge of God. For the Lord gives wisdom, and from his mouth come knowledge and understanding (Proverbs 2:3–6).

The Bible promises that God will provide wisdom so we can discern good from evil. We don't need a master's degree. We don't need to spend a few years in seminary. We don't need an IQ of 138. But we do have to pray passionately for God to bless us with wisdom and understanding, and He will supply our need.

God doesn't single out geniuses for the blessing of spiritual understanding; even so, the search for wisdom and knowledge can be intimidating. The Bible is a big book. Depending upon the version used, it can speak in a language that is almost foreign. It's filled with metaphors, imageries, and passages that sometimes seem like riddles.

Confession time: There were periods when I was a lazy student in school. I was good at what I was good at, and if I wasn't good at something, I just ignored it. Throughout my entire academic life, I had struggles with math and science, especially if it related to spatial things—geometry and physics. Being given a set of facts and having to extrapolate about something I couldn't see would spin my brain around like a top. I took home a D in high school geometry. And that was generous.

Though I had a flare for language and an ability to make complex, real world problems simple, I always thought of myself as somewhat challenged. I came from a family of strong analytical minds; I was the one whose head was always in the clouds. My sense of direction was so bad; I could get lost in my backyard. Measurement conversions, ratios, and percentages still blow my mind to Bimini. This shortcoming created in me a kind of intellectual insecurity. Before I became committed and sincere in my Christian walk, I let these deficiencies keep me from getting closer to the Bible. *How could I figure this stuff out? The language was awkward! I just didn't get it! What did it all mean?*

But God promises He will provide the Christian with understanding and wisdom (see 2 Corinthians 2:6–16). It doesn't say God only grants wisdom to professors of nuclear medicine. He will take our remedial brains and pump up the volume on our ability to understand the moral lessons He wants us to extract from the Word.

Some of the world's so-called geniuses of every generation have made careers out of denying the existence of God. There's a whole new field of science called *neurotheology* that's all about studying brain-center responses to earthly derived spiritual stimuli. Show a person a cross, then study the brain waves and see what occurs. Scientists have found similar brain responses in individuals from many different religious affiliations using many different stimuli. Some of these scientists hope to prove that God is merely a product of our thoughts, that God's very existence is nothing more than a figment of one's imagination. The reality of their findings, however, affirms that God created our brains with a capacity to worship Him by faith.

One other point: we must learn to pause before we say things that destroy and replace them with words and actions that uplift. This is a major work in progress in my own life as I fight to silence my tongue when words start riding the wind and my mouth has become seriously disconnected from my brain! We've all been there.

I remember the day a friend said to me "Oh, no!" when I announced I was pregnant with my third child. To me, of course, it was an "Oh, yes!" kind of occasion. But to the mind of this individual, I was a thirty-eight-year-old woman with two children in diapers on the brink of further complicating my life. "Oh, no!" may have been her honest gut reaction, but it still hurt because her words came at me like friendly fire.

So whether we're rushing to judge another person or carelessly using our words, we would do well to pause and *scrutinize* our thoughts and actions. This moment of scrutiny can save a lot of hurt and embarrassment and, more importantly, spare the feelings of others.

So don't forget to take that pause.

Reflections: Scrutinize!

If we cut down a mature tree, we will see layered rings of life under the bark. Each of our lives has a similar layering that goes deep beneath the surface. We must learn to strip away the top layers of our personal motivations to get at core issues involving the things we say and do. We can routinely do this by asking ourselves the following questions:

- Am I sure I have all the *facts* or am I jumping to conclusions about something?
- Why do I feel what I feel right now? What's the root cause of my frustration, anger, depression, etc.?
- Is my anger directed at the right person? Or am I punishing someone else instead?
- Why am I scared to get involved and make a difference in other people's lives? What is the risk to me? How can I help this person, even in a small way?

- Do I really need to buy this "thing" right now? Are there areas of my spending that need to be scrutinized?
- If I acquire a specific "thing," will it fix whatever's wrong with what I'm feeling inside? If so, will it change my feelings permanently or is it a temporary fix?
- Am I routinely going straight to the Bible in search of knowledge, or am I relying upon the advice of pop-culture experts?

I Is for Inspire

13

As CHRISTIAN WOMEN we must become role models of inspiration. It must be our goal to vitalize others. But what do I mean by the word, *inspire*? The dictionary defines it as: "to fill with animation, to arouse a feeling, to have an exalting influence."

Inspirational people aren't necessarily the smartest, the richest, or the most beautiful, but they have a way of using their special talents to inspire and animate others. People who are inspirational have a unique gift from God. Maybe it's courage under fire. Maybe it's the ability to make people laugh or comfort those in need. Maybe it's a knack for uplifting others with crafts or music, cooking or writing. Whatever your gift is, use it to inspire others.

I knew a woman who went to work each day with immaculately clean, pressed, and tailored clothes. Her hair was the color of milk chocolate. She always had it pulled away from her open, loving face with a little bow. I thought she looked like an exotic angel. She was a small woman who walked tall with confidence and dignity. From her Spanish-accented lips came the most beautiful tributes to God. She'd hold her head up proudly and talk about her faith and the presence of God in her life. She talked about the baby who once clung to her womb and the very sad day the doctor diagnosed Down's syndrome. She talked about the way she prayed for her unborn child and how the *miracle baby,* so named by a team of stunned doctors, emerged from her body healthy and beautiful. She quoted Scripture with the wisdom of a venerable monk. I always thought there was something out-of-this-world holy about the woman. Who was she? She was a cleaning lady. And she was a true inspiration. We don't have to be a luminary to inspire.

I spent a couple of weeks vacationing in Australia in the early 1990s. While in Sydney, I lazed around the beach for part of a day and was off in search of lunch when I came across a local diner. Inside, I struck up a conversation with Robby, an Australian transplant from Wales. I had a fascinating conversation with this fellow whom I'd just met. He felt strangely like an old, old friend. We talked for over an hour. I learned that Robby was a Vietnam veteran. He'd had a terrible blowout with his parents after the war and cut all ties with them. He figured he needed to put a couple of continents between himself and the family, so he landed in Australia where he found work as a laborer. He was the gofer for the craftsmen—the bricklayers, carpenters, and heavy equipment operators. He'd fetch them things and do essentially whatever they told him to do. Not a job that would be high on the social ladder in our country, for sure.

Anyway, in the course of our conversation, I also learned that he had many friends in Australia. His *mates* were plumbers, utility workers, and other laborers. His other mates were doctors, lawyers, and leading Australian businesspeople. I reacted with some surprise at what he was telling me, because that's not normally the social pairing I was used to seeing in my own country. Frankly, I found it hard to believe. Though he was bright and engaging, he was also covered in dust and looking very much like a man who made his living digging ditches. Hardly the kind of guy a surgeon would value, I thought.

I met Robby at his club for dinner that night. It was an elegant place with a piano bar. Many of his friends were there. And, indeed, they were doctors, lawyers, and businesspeople. They all loved Robby! The rest of my time touring Australia, I kept watch for this interesting social phenomenon. I found wherever I went that the social hierarchy in Australia is kind of an amorphous thing. In America and much of the world, we are judged mightily by what we do for a living or how much money we have. In Australia, there's something else at play. I don't pretend to know what it is, but it's not a socially discriminating society in regard to men and their friendships.

My trip to Australia had a profound effect on the way I view people. Take trash collectors as an example. We're so fortunate in this society to have people who will serve as refuse removers. These guys and gals are heroes. If it weren't for refuse collectors, I'd have to haul the stuff away myself or swim in garbage. Neither option is good. When I see a garbage truck going by and some big sweaty guy hanging off the side, I think, *You go, guy! You are performing a real service here. You have an honorable job. And I am so grateful for what you do.* Give me a choice of never seeing Brad Pitt in another movie or never having my trash picked up, I can tell you which option I would choose.

One year when we lived in Virginia, we made the refuse employees a bag of treats for Christmas. I got out on the curb and flagged them down. They looked at me as if I was going to yell at them about something. Anyway, I got their attention and handed them their treats. You would have thought I'd given them a bag of gold. From that point on, every time they emptied our trash they would walk my trash cans up the driveway and put them next to my garage door so all I had to do was drag them two feet inside. My garbage cans never blew away in the wind or got clobbered by a passing motorist. These guys took care of me, but that wasn't the reason I did it. I expected nothing in return. I just wanted to let them know that I honored their service. Their gratitude over such a simple thing told me that it wasn't often that someone gave the garbage collectors more than a passing glance, and these guys are the service workers supreme. It would not be a pleasant world without them.

Inspirational people look for the good in bad situations and do not allow themselves to be poisoned by cynicism and negativity. My friend, Dea, is someone whose nurturing and supportive nature has lifted me at times I've needed encouragement. She helps out with the boys on occasion so Todd and I can go out to dinner. One day, I took Dea to our television set to show her how to operate the VCR. Standing about two and a half feet from the screen, I noticed a mosaic of grubby little handprints and a little layer of grime. I felt myself flush tomato red.

"Oh, Dea!" I said. "Look at that dust! I am so ashamed!"

With a gentle tone and loving twinkle in her eyes, Dea replied, "Don't you find that dust and things just kind of blow into your house when the weather warms up?"

Now, I knew that I hadn't wiped my television screen in six months. Dea, no doubt, suspected as much, but being a beautifully inspirational person, she had words of comfort for me. She knew that as a full-time, at-home mother I was stretched as thin as a yanked rubber band, and she seized an opportunity to lift me up. I will never forget her kind, soothing words delivered at a time I seriously needed a boost.

Inspirational people also know when to seize windows of opportunity to share their faith. My friend Linda and her husband, Don, are devout Christians whose joy in the Lord could light up a cave. Don is a man who's smart, lovable, and at times, hysterically funny. He has an approachable, disarming quality that allows him to make Jesus come to life in the lives of people who are new to the faith.

Linda, who's petite, soft-spoken, and lovely would be the first to tell you that she and Don are total opposites. He's out there on the front lines with the big hugs and pithy one-liners. She's looking for a chair toward the back of the room.

"It's not easy for me," Linda related, "to get up in front of large groups and talk. This takes me way out of my comfort zone."

Without having to shout from the rooftop, Linda has found her own way to witness for God. She does this through what she calls "through me" opportunities.

"I've been blessed with these quiet moments," she said, "where I can share a story about my own life's experience as it relates to my faith and turn these occasions into opportunities to lead others to God." Linda says she prays for these moments to happen.

One such incident occurred at Don and Linda's house shortly after September 11th. Linda was at home when the man came to install one of Don's massive aquariums. As the serviceman worked on the tank, they made some small talk. He asked about Linda's family and found out her boys were now grown. Finally, the conversation turned to September 11th and the ensuing war on terror. He asked Linda if she was worried about the potential for a military draft that would pull her civilian boys into an ugly war. Linda said she thought for a moment and then went to the Lord with a small prayer that He would embolden her to say the right things. Then she thoughtfully gave this man what she calls a "through me" reply.

Linda told him that her faith in Jesus has taken away those kinds of worries and fears. She related that with Jesus at the center of her life, the uncertainties are all but gone.

Linda said the man, who had been working as he was talking, abruptly stopped what he was doing. With some emotion he told her that he had strayed from the church and only recently returned to give his faith another try.

"It's as if the words that God gave me touched this man at the right time, and I was grateful to God for the chance to witness my faith," Linda recounted.

Linda isn't publicly speaking to throngs for God, but in her own quiet way, she is a woman of amazing inspiration who is touching the lives of the people she encounters every day of her life.

God used Linda in a wonderful way to inspire me as I was looking for a book publisher. AMG Publishers had just proposed a contract on this book. I had done a bit of research on AMG early on and was delighted with the company's mission focus, which extends to orphanages worldwide. I had also developed a great working relationship with the manager of acquisitions, Dan Penwell. I found him to be a person of great heart, humor, and wisdom. When the contract landed in my hands, it should have been one of the happiest days of my life, the start of a new and exciting journey. But something on the periphery of this experience was casting shadows as elements of my life began to veer off course. These were areas I held most dear—my husband, my children, and my church.

Around the time that I was offered the contract, I began to notice my children's rivalries and their bickering began to terribly annoy me. I've always tried to be patient and loving with my boys. I've bitten my lip to the color purple on many occasions to keep harsh and heated words from penetrating little ears. But I was now becoming quick-tempered over trivial matters; spilled milk could flash me to the moon. I was feeling resentful and edgy toward Todd. I picked a fight with him during vacation and used some choice words that were anything but Christian to dredge up and pick at old wounds. I even began to feel some disillusionment with our church. One Sunday when Todd was out of town on a business trip, I packed the kids in the car and set out to search for a different place to worship.

One morning, I woke up with heaviness in my heart and felt an urge to call Linda. A few days later, I set out for the local McDonald's where Linda and I talked while the boys ran about the play area. I poured out a river of grievances that afternoon as we both picked at our salads and burgers, too absorbed in conversation to really eat. When I was finished, I felt as if I'd unburdened myself of about ten tons of dead weight. Then it was time for Linda to talk. She leaned forward slightly and locked my eyes with hers in a look that told me something big was coming.

"You have to understand," she said very carefully, "that you are under *attack*." I could feel the hair lift on my arms, as I immediately understood the implication of what she was saying.

"Satan doesn't want this book published," she said. "I wish I could tell you that it's going to get better before it gets worse."

"Be careful," she continued, "because he's going to hit you where you're most vulnerable."

Flashing in my mind were snapshots of my husband, my three little boys, and the church I used to love. I knew then, with 100 percent certainty, who and what was behind this recent and mysteriously intense downward drift in my life. I understood why it happened to coincide with a major step forward in publishing a very frank book about sin. It was as if God worked through Linda that day to warn me about the evil one.

The woman of inspiration is the woman within each of us. It's just getting to her that's the challenge. The *inspirational woman* is the woman who always has something nice to say about the neighbor no one else likes. The *inspirational woman* is the woman who gives an hour of her busy week to serve at the local soup kitchen. The *inspirational woman* is the woman who brings a homeless man a brown bag lunch. The *inspirational woman* is the woman who lets the nervous minivan driver merge into her lane on a car-creeping highway after a dozen other motorists refused to give an inch. The *inspirational woman* is the woman who keeps her lips quiet long enough to let others talk. The *inspirational woman* is the woman who lets other people soak up the moments of glory without trying to steal the stage. The *inspirational woman* is the woman who gives something of herself freely without being asked. The *inspirational woman* becomes a role model for others by virtue of the things she does in her life that lift people up—the small things that glorify God.

Reflections: Inspire!

Do an Inspiration Inventory on a week in your life. Take note of what you say and do in your everyday conversations with others, including your spouse and other family members. You don't have to document every conversation, but jot down your impressions of the interactions you have with others. Use a simple homemade checklist, such as this:

- How do I rate my dealings and encounters with
  _____ (family, friend, acquaintance)?
  - Mostly Positive?
  - Neutral?
  - Mostly Negative?
- After keeping the inventory for a week, does a pattern emerge? Are my encounters heavily leaning in the direction of one particular category?
- Are there specific relationships that are receiving a "mostly negative" mark? Is there something different I could do to improve and strengthen those relationships?
- What changes can I make, with God's help, to make most of my encounters "positive?"

N Is for Neutralize

14

N<small>EUTRALIZE</small> THE OPPOSITION, or as the dictionary defines it, "make the opposition ineffective." It does indeed take two to tango. So stop dancing. Quit competing with your friends and neighbors. Nullify the competitive instincts by refusing to play the game. Do this in a loving, friendly manner and you will forge deeper, truly meaningful bonds with those around you.

In chapter 5, there was a dialogue among two friends: Mary Jane and Sally Ann. Remember them? They were chatting on the phone about clothes and they ended up fencing with one another over who has the best taste in shopping venues.

With a mind for neutralizing the opposition, let's try that conversation again.

(Ring! Ring! Mary Jane's giving her pal Sally Ann a jingle.)

Mary Jane: Hi! I just got back from K-Mart. I picked up the cutest little pair of shorts.

Sally Ann: *(the subtle put-down)* Really! That's great. Actually, I was at Nordstrom's last week and I picked up a few things for myself. I just love that store!

Mary Jane: *(doesn't play the game)* I know what you mean! Hey, how was Ben's soccer camp?

Sally Ann: *(realizes she can't brag about her clothes, so she tries to boast about her son)* Oh, it was great! He is such a natural athlete.

Mary Jane: *(doesn't spar . . . she's out of the game)* You are so blessed. I'm glad it went so well.

When Sally Ann prattles on about the stores she goes to we must resist the temptation to come back with something bigger and better. Avoid justifying or defending. Simply get off the subject, not angrily or abruptly. Politely acknowledge whatever Sally Ann has just said and move on. Stay positive and resist the temptation to come back with: "But-wait-until-you-hear-about-this" statements. When I am tempted to boast about something, I remind myself of this: I would rather be *liked* than *envied*. This helps me keep shallow and potentially destructive words from rolling off my lips!

Let's face it: women are competitive. How do we peacefully coexist? What if the trappings of vanity are all around you? What if your gorgeous friends and their extravagant, debt-ridden lifestyles are constantly pecking away at you? Find a way to *neutralize* them. Let them know graciously but in no uncertain terms that you are not competing with anyone but yourself. When you stop competing with them, they will stop competing with you. And you will both be liberated.

The apostle Paul says this about the vain game: "Let us not become conceited, provoking and envying each other" (Galatians 5:26). The use of the word *provoking* is interesting, because that's exactly what we do when we enter into a competition with other women over vanities. Sally Ann provokes Mary Jane. Mary Jane may become envious. She provokes Sally Ann in return. On and on it goes in a never-ending, toxic loop.

The apostle Paul gives us a bit of insight into the futility of competition: "When they measure themselves by themselves and compare themselves with themselves, they are not wise" (2 Corinthians 10:12). Our competitive nature can influence our dreams for the future. How many of us have pinned our hopes and desires on the day we finally possess that bigger and better house in that bigger and better neighborhood? I recently saw a commercial that showed a happy young couple skipping past a "For Sale" sign on the front yard of a beautiful, white house. The voice-over spun dreamy words around the subject of "the promotion" as the lovely pair glided by. The point being, of course: we're going to run out and buy a new house once we get that job promotion! That's what a promotion is for, right? And how many of us take life's good fortunes—the promotions, the bonuses, the unexpected financial gifts—and immediately go out and upgrade the material dimension of our lives? We get a new car. We move into a bigger house. We buy a bunch of new furniture. But in doing so, we are creating for ourselves a cycle of dependency. This dependency has chained many of us to jobs we hate. We've bought ourselves into a socioeconomic lifestyle we can't afford to abandon. The end result: we've become competitive with those around us and we may not even realize it.

I was walking around the downstairs floor of my home noticing how my children's toys had seemingly mutated and multiplied overnight. Playroom toys—some in duplicate and triplicate—were carelessly cast about every room. I shook my head as I walked from room to room and wondered to myself how we had managed to let these playthings infect and overrun our house. The task of cleaning up was no small job. Though I recruited the aid of the little munchkins who had made this big mess, it was a huge effort getting everything back where it belonged. That night I said to Todd, "I want a smaller house the next time we move. I need less space." Long term, I want to downgrade and *simplify* because I've learned that there's little peace or happiness associated with the care and maintenance of a house filled with *things*. When my children no longer need a backyard in which to run and spaces to contain their toys and gear, I want to streamline my life. It's a case, to my thinking, where less is truly more.

I wrote about Texas artist Ann Hardy and her love of adventure in chapter 5. Ann has a lovely estate that overlooks a creek near our neighborhood. The home and its backdrop are breathtakingly beautiful. Every time I pass her house, I mentally sigh. But it's not the house or the backyard that makes me crane my neck and nearly drive into a ditch every time I pass, it's the little tree house out back. Yes, it's Ann's tree house that I covet.

Ann had a tree house built, and it is from this whimsical vantage that she paints. She has a lovely home overlooking a peaceful, idyllic landscape, but she retreats to a small house in a tree to dream and create. When I see people around me upgrade and bloat themselves into a state of utter dependence upon high-paying jobs, I think, maybe all I really need is a tree house in my backyard. As a Christian woman, I must stop putting my goals and dreams into a material basket that's going to leave me feeling empty when it's full.

So get out of the game, but do keep this in mind: getting out of the game isn't about moving to some faraway island and surrounding ourselves by big barking dogs and a moat. As many Christian women step deeper into the spiritual journey, there's a nesting phenomenon that often takes place. God recognizes the earnest quest. He begins to reveal more knowledge, and pretty soon, the big old world isn't looking too good. What this does to many people is drive them into a Christian bubble. They insulate themselves. They "nest." They get rid of old friends. They yank their kids out of public schools and send them to private schools or do homeschooling. Private schools can be outstanding and homeschooling is a wonderful alternative. (Some of the brightest, most spiritually grounded children I've ever encountered are products of homeschool environments.) But the cumulative effect of all of these distancing tactics means the Christians are only communing with themselves. This becomes a selfish pursuit that is anything but Christian in practice.

Recently, I was at lunch with a group of parents and children from my oldest son's school. As we laughed, talked, and bonded over the shared love of our faith and families, I wanted to pinch myself for the blessings of this wonderful group. Then the smile left my face, as I contemplated what I'd done recently in the way of interacting with and supporting people outside my faith—not much! I caught myself in an extended period of nesting in that comfortable and safe Christian bubble.

Jesus, in contrast, remained very much in the world. He befriended prostitutes and the people on the other side of the tracks. Jesus didn't cut himself off from the world. He had to be *in* the world to do His job. And if we Christians cut ourselves off from the non-Christian world, we are missing vital opportunities to spread the faith. Notice how Jesus connected with the world:

> While Jesus was having dinner at Levi's house, many tax collectors and 'sinners' were eating with him and his disciples, for there were many who followed him. When the teachers of the law who were Pharisees saw him eating with the 'sinners' and tax collectors, they asked his disciples: "Why does he eat with tax collectors and 'sinners'?" On hearing this, Jesus said to them, "It is not the healthy who need a doctor, but the sick. I have not come to call the righteous, but sinners" (Mark 2:15–17).

Jesus was able to *neutralize,* to make the opposition ineffective by becoming involved with them. There was no pretense, no vanity, no competition. He was God/man on their playing field. That's what being a witness for God is all about! It's about getting the word out to the people who need it the most! It's about connecting with people.

Reflections: Neutralize!

When I find myself battling for airtime in the company of someone who wants to spar and I am tempted to compete, I default in my mind to an old but effective cliché: "Bite your lip!" This helps remind me that I'm dealing with someone who's going to drag me down a path that's not spiritually nourishing.

- When I am in a situation involving verbal competition, how am I most likely to respond? Do I spar, or do I avoid saying things that fuel the competition?
- Reflecting upon the times I have sparred, how do I feel about the encounter afterward? How do I feel about myself afterward?
- Thinking about the times I have "bitten my lip," how do I feel about the encounter afterward? How do I feel about myself afterward?

I encourage you to come up with your own mental *neutralizer*—a statement that you can call upon to help you "bite your lip" in those frustrating competitive situations. Plan to employ this the next time you encounter someone who wants to "one up" you and experience peace and comfort as you step outside the sparring ring!

The Final Word

AFTER COMPLETING the first draft of this book, I was dogged with the sense that something was missing. Then one night at a Bible study meeting, I knew what it was. We were talking in a small group about the difficulty of shedding our "old nature" in our daily Christian lives. One of the group members, a man, related how hard it was to control his appetite.

"I feel like I am in control of most aspects of my life," he said. "But when it comes to food, I have no willpower. If someone sets a box of doughnuts in front of me, I don't stop at one. I am powerless when it comes to food."

173

I listened to the sadness in his voice and I watched his wife's reaction to what he was saying. Her face registered help-lessness and pain. Then I realized that I was sitting on a secret. God had given me something this man desired—the strength to overcome temptation as it relates to food. I knew then that I had to share my testimony with this man and his wife. I also knew what needed to happen with my book. The missing piece was all about my years as a bulimic—something I had shared with only a few people.

As the Bible class was letting out, I went over to that man and his wife. "I have something I want to share with you," I said. My voice was shaking and my heart was pounding because I was about to step into an area of con-fession where I had never before gone. I was about to let it all hang out with people I hardly knew. There was the potential now for exposure, but God whispered that the time was right.

"I used to have a problem with food," I told the man. "I could eat a box of doughnuts just like you."

"But you don't have a weight problem," the wife said with a puzzled look.

"That's because I was eating doughnuts and then forcing myself to throw up," I said.

There was a reflective pause, then I watched the lines on their faces soften, and the walls came tumbling down.

I went on to share my testimony that night. It was a difficult thing to do, but I was comforted greatly by the reaction. There was none of the disgust or distancing I always imagined would occur if anyone ever knew my secret. This incident gave me the courage to begin opening up with others.

Over the next several weeks, this scenario played out in my life again and again as I shared my story. I began with new friends, because they only knew the healthy me and it was easier to talk about a problem I had when they had not known me. The task was harder with old friends because I was about to share with people who *did* know me during the problem years. They would discover that I had been living a lie. I wondered if they would feel betrayed, but something poignant began to happen.

People began to open up about their own lives. I learned about struggles and burdens and pain in the lives of friends who began to share their own stories. I was touched and inspired by the way in which others have endured and overcome battles that were even larger and more emotionally scarring than my own.

So this anxiety I'd carried around for so many years about how people would view me in light of my own past was all just wasted, empty fear. The people who used to love me still loved me. And friends, old and new, now know the real me. Hidden secrets that built walls of shame are coming into the light, and we are free at last to know the depth of genuine friendship and love.

It's an exciting time in my life. I feel as if God is connecting the dots as I grow and mature in Him. The Bible tells us that God works through broken vessels. In my own life, He has taken the shattered pieces of my life and restored the parts to make me whole.

I shared a final draft of this manuscript with one of my new friends not long ago. After she finished reading it, she hugged me tightly and I could see tears in her eyes.

"I'm so sorry," she said, "for everything you've been through."

"I look back at some of the worst moments," I replied, "and I realize there were lessons to be learned. I am truly grateful for where I've been because it's given me an unshakable faith and appreciation for life."

I have a long way to go in my spiritual walk. I continue to battle many of the sins I write about in this book. But, through God's palpable presence in my life and His Word, I have been blessed with an eye-opening window into the real me. The picture is not always pretty and I am far from perfect. But, by the grace of God, I am now aware. And this is an important step on the road to where we all long to be in the end—with God and worthy in His sight.

May God bless you and keep you safe and secure in His love, always.

Endnotes

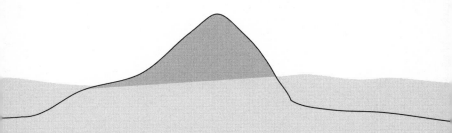

1. Michael E. Young, "A Friend in Deed," Page 1A, *The Dallas Morning News* (23 April 2001).

2. Jacquielynn Floyd, "He Knows to Respect His Elders," Page 15A, *The Dallas Morning News* (17 April 2001).

3. Bergen Evans, *Dictionary of Quotations* (New York: Bonanza Books, Division of Crown Books, Inc. 1968), 773.

If this book has touched your heart,
please share it with a friend.

You can visit Sarah at www.sarahonderdonk.com

Your feedback is a blessing.